I AM THE GOD THAT REVEALS

PATRICIA L. ELLIOTT

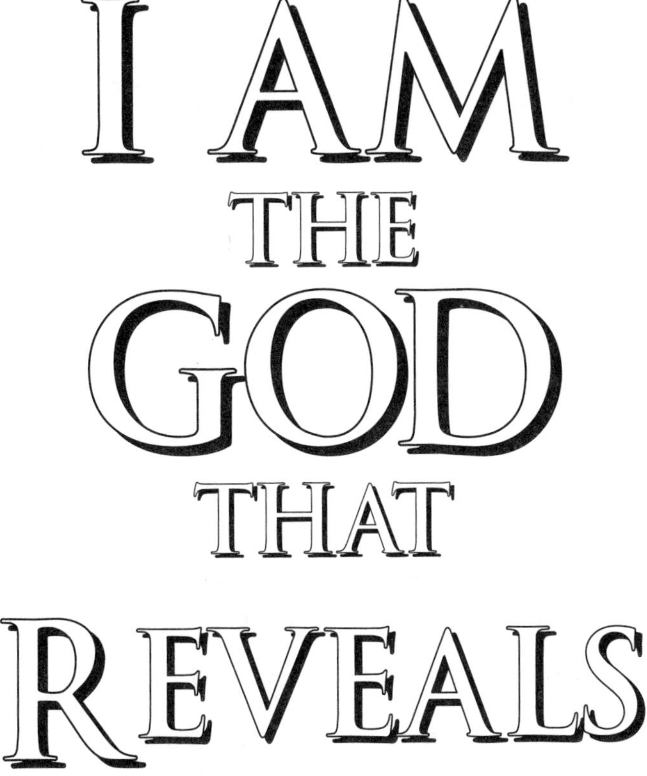

I AM THE GOD THAT REVEALS

Unveiling of Revelation

VMI PUBLISHERS • SISTERS, OREGON

Published by
VMI Publishers
Sisters, Oregon
www.vmipublishers.com

ISBN 10: 1-933204-91-5
ISBN 13: 978-1-933204-91-8

Library of Congress: 2009926352

Cover design by Rebecca Barbier

This book is dedicated to the glory and honor of the
Lord Jesus Christ,
who paid such a dear price to rescue my soul.

Yeshua,
My heart overflows with such deep gratitude.
I love You with all my heart, with all my soul, and
with all my strength.

Your Amah,
Patricia

Contents

Prologue

It is with holy reverential fear and love of the Lord God Almighty that I place my pen to the paper and begin what seems to be a monumental task. But in fact, the Lord promised me that this book on Revelation would be an easy undertaking as He whispered these words in my ear: "*For this is My work and it is never burdensome nor heavy.*"

For several months, the Holy Spirit placed an unquenchable thirst within me to understand the prophetic books of Ezekiel, Daniel, Zechariah, and Revelation. The Lord instructed me to read these books and while studying them His words to me were: "*You will get a fuller revelation of these prophetic books when I show you in the Spirit events that will take place. I have placed it within your heart to understand the mysteries of My Holy Word written by My prophets.* When I completed my studies on the books of Ezekiel, Daniel, and Zechariah, the Holy Spirit instructed me to study the book of Revelation. The Lord impressed upon my heart to read a section of Scripture and then to pray in my prayer language, and while I prayed in tongues the Holy Spirit opened up my understanding of Revelation. It is with His understanding that was imparted to me that I write this book. I have included the Lord's words to me in italics because they contain His explanation of Holy Scriptures and I never want to take credit for what the Holy Spirit of God has revealed. All glory and honor belong to Jesus Christ because the book of Revelation is His revelation to the church.

While writing this book, the Lord humbled His handmaiden when He reminded me of this: "*My Word is powerful. One of My words is more powerful than one thousand of yours. When you quote My Holy Word, power goes forth to convict and change hearts.*" "For the word of God is living and powerful, sharper than any two-edged sword, piercing even to the division of the soul and spirit, and of the joints and marrow, and is a discerner of the thoughts and intents of the heart" (Hebrews 4:12).

My prayer is that this book will open the eyes of your understanding to the Revelation of Jesus Christ. Jesus earnestly desires His church to be prepared for these end time events, because if we are not, even His elect could be deceived. Jesus gave His church this warning. "Then if anyone says to you, 'Look, here is the Christ!' or 'There!' do not believe it. For false christs and false prophets will rise and show great signs and wonders to deceive, if possible, even the elect. See I have told you beforehand" (Matthew 24:23–25).

Introduction

Throughout the history of mankind, God's sovereignty has been displayed by how He chooses to reveal who He is and when He chooses to reveal His divine plan for man. God walked and talked with Adam and Eve face to face until their sin separated them from His presence. From that point forward, God no longer physically dwelt with His people, but still spoke to them in a way that they had no doubt that it was God speaking. God confronted Cain about murdering his brother; He gave Noah specific instructions on building the ark, and He told Abraham to leave his native country because He was giving him a land of promise that would make him into a great nation. God revealed Himself to Moses in the burning bush by identifying Himself and His plan for the Israelites. "And God said to Moses, "I AM WHO I AM." And He said, "Thus you shall say to the children of Israel, 'I AM has sent me to you'" (Exodus 3:14). God chose to reveal His plans through His servants the prophets in the Old Testament. "Surely the Lord GOD does nothing, unless He reveals His secret to His servants the prophets" (Amos 3:7). Through Isaiah, God made His name known and promised to make known future events before they happened.

> I am the LORD, that is My name;
> And My glory I will not give to another,
> Nor My praise to carved images.

Behold, the former things have come to pass,
And new things I declare;
Before they spring forth I tell you of them.
(Isaiah 42:8–9)

The prophet Joel said there would come a day when God would pour out His Spirit on all men and women and that God would reveal His plans through prophecy, dreams and visions.

And it shall come to pass afterward
That I will pour out My Spirit on all flesh;
Your sons and your daughters shall prophesy,
Your old men shall dream dreams,
Your young men shall see visions.
And also on My menservants and on My maidservants
I will pour out My Spirit in those days.
(Joel 2:28–29)

The next time in history that God chose to walk face to face with man on earth and reveal His plan was through the Messiah Jesus Christ. Before Jesus ascended into heaven after His resurrection, He told His disciples to wait in Jerusalem for the promise of the Father. "But you shall receive power when the Holy Spirit has come upon you; and you shall be witnesses to Me in Jerusalem, and in all Judea and Samaria, and to the end of the earth" (Acts 1:8). On the day of Pentecost that promise was fulfilled when the Holy Spirit descended upon the one hundred and twenty gathered in the upper room, and they began to speak the gospel in languages they had never learned. In one of the greatest evangelistic messages ever delivered, Peter identified this phenomenon as the fulfillment of the Spirit of God being poured out that the prophet Joel had spoken about.

The Holy Spirit was given to us by God the Father through Jesus

Christ so that He could be our Guide and our Comforter. He is the voice of God to direct our paths to gain understanding and knowledge of who God is and God's divine plan for man. The Holy Spirit is the One who decides how He will reveal God to us; we don't get to choose. Since Pentecost, great men of God have recorded in the New Testament how the Holy Spirit imparts these revelations to man. I want to focus on three specific ways that the Holy Spirit uses to reveal God's plan because these are how His revelations came to me for this book. The Holy Spirit showed me future events that would take place through visions, His inner voice spoken to me during those visions and through praying in the Spirit using my prayer language. With my eyes closed, the Holy Spirit would form pictures that I could see, and then with His inner voice He would explain to me what I was viewing. Sometimes I would see a scene like a clip from a movie and I just knew by His Spirit what I saw. Still, other times I would read Scripture, pause, and then pray in tongues. While praying in tongues, the Holy Spirit would open up the eyes of my understanding of that Scripture. These are biblical means that the Holy Spirit employs to communicate God's will, His way, and His plan and are validated by these Scriptures.

> Now there was a certain disciple at Damascus named Ananias; and to him the Lord said in a vision, "Ananias." And he said, "Here I am, Lord." So the Lord said to him, "Arise and go to the street called Straight, and inquire at the house of Judas for one called Saul of Tarsus, for behold, he is praying. And in a vision he has seen a man named Ananias coming in and putting his hand on him, so that he might receive his sight. (Acts 9:10–12)
>
> And a vision appeared to Paul in the night. A man of Macedonia stood and pleaded with him, saying, "Come over to Macedonia and help us." Now after he had seen the vision, immediately we sought to go to Macedonia, concluding that the Lord had called us to preach the gospel to them. (Acts 16:9–10)

The Holy Spirit gave Ananias and Paul visions and God revealed His plans to them as a result of their seeking Him in prayer. A dedicated prayer life is of utmost importance in discerning and receiving the things of God. Jude said that praying in tongues builds up our faith to receive things from the Holy Spirit, and Paul said that we should always be praying in the Spirit. "But you, beloved, building yourselves up on your most holy faith, praying in the Holy Spirit" (Jude 20). "…Praying always with all prayer and supplication in the Spirit, being watchful to this end with all perseverance and supplication for all the saints…" (Ephesians 6:18). Paul also said that when we pray in tongues no one understands, but we are speaking the mysteries of God. As we utter those mysteries to God, the Holy Spirit can reveal them to our understanding. This is how the Holy Spirit opened up the Scriptures of Revelation to me. "For he who speaks in a tongue does not speak to men but to God, for no one understands him; however, in the spirit he speaks mysteries" (1 Corinthians 14:2).

I did not decide to write this book. God divinely called me to write it. I chose to obey. I did not choose how these events would be revealed to me or what events would be revealed to me; the Holy Spirit did. I did not select the time, the day, or the place that these events and messages were revealed; God did. Some were revealed while I was in Israel, some were revealed while studying Scriptures outside on my deck; some were revealed while worshipping the Lord in song; some were revealed at a secluded place of solitude where I spend time one–on-one with the Lord; and some were revealed as I was waking from a deep sleep. These visions, messages from the Lord, and great understanding of Scriptures came through the Holy Spirit over a period of a year while I studied and wrote this book on Revelation. God deserves all the glory, honor, and praise for this work is truly His. I am just His handmaiden whom He chose for this task.

Chapter One

Open Your Ears

Revelation 1:1–9

The Revelation of Jesus Christ, which God gave Him to show His servants—things which must shortly take place. And He sent and signified it by His angel to His servant John, who bore witness to the word of God, and to the testimony of Jesus Christ, to all things that he saw. Blessed is he who reads and those who hear the words of this prophecy, and keep those things which are written in it; for the time is near."

John, to the seven churches which are in Asia: Grace to you and peace from Him who is and who was and who is to come, and from the seven Spirits who are before His throne, and from Jesus Christ, the faithful witness, the firstborn from the dead, and the ruler over the kings of the earth. To Him who loved us and washed us from our sins in His own blood, and has made us kings and priests to His God and Father, to Him be glory and dominion forever and ever. Amen. Behold, He is coming with clouds, and every eye will see Him, even they who pierced Him. And all the tribes of the earth will mourn because of Him. Even so, Amen. "I am the Alpha and the Omega, the Beginning and the End," says the Lord "who is and who was and who is to come, the Almighty."

I, John, both your brother and companion in the tribulation and kingdom and patience of Jesus Christ, was on the island that

> is called Patmos for the word of God and for the testimony of Jesus Christ.

The book of Revelation is the only book in the Bible that promises a blessing to those who read the book, who hear the words and who keep the things which are written. The Greek word for hear is *akouo* which means to come to the ears by being reported in such a way that there is understanding. Those that gain an understanding of the book of Revelation and take heed to the message will be blessed. Dear reader, upon completion of this book, you will have read the entire book of Revelation and have a greater comprehension of Jesus' final words to His church before He returns. All that remains for the blessing to be yours is to obey the words that Jesus Christ has given you.

John rehearsed central truths about Jesus and summed them up with meticulous precision so that the reader would know that Jesus was the promised Messiah; the same one who appeared to him on Patmos. A central truth that John wanted to convey was Jesus' eternal nature which makes Him God. Next, he wanted his readers to know that this was the same Jesus that he witnessed being crucified on the cross and who rose from the dead. Jesus came to this earth the first time to shed His blood to wash away our sins and to give us His authority as priests and kings. In the Old Testament there was no higher authority in the land than the king and no higher authority in the temple than the high priest. Through Jesus' death and resurrection, He regained dominion over the earthly realm and the spiritual realm that was given to Satan as a result of Adam and Eve's sin. Before Jesus ascended into to Heaven, He delegated this authority back to man, namely the believer in Christ, and that is the reason we are called priests and kings. Another fundamental truth that John's readers needed to know was the certainty that Jesus will come again the second time. He will appear in the clouds and everyone will know that He is the Messiah from His pierced hands and feet. There will be a deep mourning on the earth when every eye sees His wounds and the realization sinks in that Jesus Christ was the promised Savior.

The seven Spirits that are before the throne of God require an explanation. Who are these Spirits and what is their purpose? We know from these verses that these seven Spirits are not Jesus. The Holy Spirit is ministering on the earth, so they cannot be the Holy Spirit. In Revelation chapter four, these seven Spirits are identified as the Spirits of God, and Isaiah identifies the seven Spirits which also reveals their function within the church. "Seven lamps of fire were burning before the throne, which are the seven Spirits of God" (Revelation 4:5).

> There come forth a Rod from the stem of Jesse,
> And a Branch shall grow out of His roots.
> The Spirit of the LORD shall rest upon Him,
> The Spirit of wisdom and understanding,
> The Spirit of counsel and might,
> The spirit of knowledge and the fear of the *LORD*.
> (Isaiah 11:1–2 Emphasis added)

The seven Spirits of God that Isaiah identified are the Spirit of the LORD, the Spirit of wisdom, the Spirit of understanding, the Spirit of counsel, the Spirit of might, the Spirit of knowledge, and the Spirit of the fear of the LORD. In order to fully comprehend the message that Jesus Christ gave to the seven churches in Asia Minor, these seven Spirits of God will play an integral part of that revelation and will be discussed. The correlation between the seven Spirits of God and the seven churches in Asia Minor were revealed to me by the Holy Spirit. *"Child, because of your diligence in studying My Word, I have opened up to you things that you do not know."* The Seven Spirits of God have a specific message for the seven churches that Jesus addressed and also for churches today.

The Apostle John had been exiled to the Island of Patmos, which was a small island in the Aegean Sea off the coast of Asia Minor. The seven churches that John wrote to in the book of Revelation were all located in Asia Minor, which is current day Turkey. John was exiled to this island at a time when the Christian church was experiencing great tribulation from the hands of a cruel Roman ruler. Bible scholars believe that the book of Revelation was written between A.D. 81–96, and Domitian would have been that Roman ruler who executed his cruel hand upon the Christians. It was a capital crime to be connected with the church and it was a custom to put an accused Christian to the test by requiring him to sacrifice to the image of the emperor. There was much bloody persecution, which resulted in the torture and death of multitudes of Christians who refused to worship the godhead of Domitian. He was the first of the Roman emperors to deify himself during his lifetime by assuming the title of "Lord and God." Domitian was also known to exile his enemies that posed a threat to him. The Apostle John would have been a formidable enemy because Domitian is said to have placed John in boiling oil, but he was divinely delivered from death by God. Since Domitian couldn't silence John by killing him, he exiled him to a remote island for the Word of God and for his testimony of Jesus Christ. God delivered John from death because his work for the Lord was not yet finished, for the book of Revelation was penned during his exile on the island of Patmos.

REVELATION 1:10–20

> I was in the Spirit on the Lord's Day, and I heard behind me a loud voice, as of a trumpet, saying, "I am the Alpha and the Omega, the First and the Last," and, "What you see, write in a book and send it to the seven churches which are in Asia: to Ephesus, to Smyrna, to Pergamos, to Thyatira, to Sardis, to Philadelphia, and to Laodicea." Then I turned to see the voice that spoke with me. And having turned I saw seven golden lampstands, and in the midst of the seven lampstands One like the Son of Man, clothed with a garment down to the feet and girded about the chest with a golden band. His head and hair were white like wool, as white as snow,

> and His eyes like a flame of fire; His feet were like fine brass, as if refined in a furnace, and His voice as the sound of many waters; He had in His right hand seven stars, out of His mouth went a sharp two-edged sword, and His countenance was like the sun shining in its strength. And when I saw Him, I fell at His feet as dead. But He laid His right hand on me, saying to me, "Do not be afraid; I am the First and the Last. I am He who lives, and was dead, and behold, I am alive forevermore. Amen. And I have the keys of Hades and of Death. Write the things which you have seen, and the things which are, and the things which will take place after this. The mystery of the seven stars which you saw in My right hand, and the seven golden lampstands: The seven stars are the angels of the seven churches, and the seven lampstands which you saw are the seven churches.

John's exile on a remote island afforded him a lot of time to pray in the Spirit and seek the Lord's direction for himself and for the church that he so dearly loved and guided throughout his lifetime. Sometimes I think we all should be sent to an uninhabited island where there are no TV's, Internet, phones, or other distracting forms of technology, so we can get alone with God to hear His voice. All the distractions of John's life were divinely removed and while he was in the Spirit, he heard a loud voice calling out to him to write everything he saw and to place it in a book. When John turned to see who had spoken to Him, the sight of this powerful Son of man caused him to wither to the ground as a lifeless rag. The commanding presence of Jesus Christ humbled John and prepared him to receive extraordinary revelations from the Son of God. I have always wanted to have an experience like John and see Jesus face to face before I take my last breath on earth. Maybe being flat on my face in holy reverential fear of the Lord God Almighty is what this Bible-toting evangelist with a PhD needs to keep her humble. The Lord was adamant about my remaining humble in light of the great things that He revealed to me for this book. *"I will show you great and mighty things. You must remain humble or pride will be your downfall. Get on your face and pray."* Through the Word of God, the Holy Spirit has given me the Lord's remedy for remaining a humble servant of the Lord. "Therefore humble yourselves under the mighty hand of God, that He may exalt you in due time, casting all your care upon Him, for He cares for you" (1 Peter 5:6-7). A key factor of true humility is an admission that you need God to take care of you. By placing all your anxieties and day-to-day cares upon Him and trusting that He will see you through, you are acknowledging your profound dependence upon God. Pride says I can do this myself, but humility says I desperately need help from God. "If My people who are called by My name will humble themselves, and pray and seek My face, and turn from their wicked ways, then I will hear from heaven, and will forgive their sin and heal their land" (2 Chronicles 7:14). Humility means having an intimate relationship with the Lord so that you can seek God through prayer to know His will. It is not enough to know the will of God; you must be prepared to change what He shows you about yourself. When He shows you sin in your life, repentance and asking for His forgiveness keeps you humble. "My soul shall make its boast in the LORD; the humble shall hear of it and be glad" (Psalm 34:2). Boasting in the Lord and proclaiming His goodness, mercy, love, and provisions in our lives is a sure way to remain humble. Those who are truly humble will rejoice in the wonderful ways that God has provided for them. But those who are full of pride will always boast about their accomplishments and their success without ever mentioning God's hand in it. Micah says that to walk humbly before God, we must make proper daily decisions that are honorable and reflect understanding, compassion, and forgiveness. "He has shown you, O man, what is good; and what does the LORD require of you but to do justly, to love mercy, and to walk humbly with your God?" (Micah 6:8). Our response and treatment of others will reflect whether we are truly people of humility, or whether we are filled with pride. "Likewise you younger people, submit yourselves to your elders. Yes, all of you be submissive to one another, and be clothed with humility, for "God resists the proud, but gives grace to the humble" (1 Peter 5:5). Jesus' appearance to John surely humbled him, but with this humbling came a lifting up. Jesus placed His right hand upon John and told him not to be afraid. With the touch of Jesus, John's fear was removed, his strength was restored, and he was ready to be commissioned to document God's plan for humanity. He was told to record what he saw and to send it to the seven churches, and over 1900 years later the churches are still reading it! How amazing the touch of God is upon a humble servant of the Lord because in due time, He will lift you up.

The words that Jesus used to describe Himself spoke of His nature and His finished work. "I am the Alpha and Omega, the First and the Last" spoke of His eternal nature. "I am He who lives, and was dead, and behold I am alive forever more" spoke of His virgin birth, His death on the cross and His resurrection from the dead. "And I have the keys of Hades and death" is described in the story that Jesus told in the gospel of Luke of the rich man and Lazarus. Although Jesus taught in many parables, this was not a parable but a true account that described the place where the unrighteous and the righteous dead went upon death before Calvary. Hades was on one side of a great fixed gulf and Abraham's bosom, or Paradise, was on the other side.

> There was a certain rich man who was clothed in purple and fine linen and fared sumptuously every day. But there was a certain beggar named Lazarus, full of sores, who was laid at his gate, desiring to be fed with the crumbs which fell from the rich man's table. Moreover the dogs came and licked his sores. So it was that the beggar died, and was carried by the angels to Abraham's bosom. The rich man also died and was buried. And being in torments in Hades, he lifted up his eyes and saw Abraham afar off, and Lazarus in his bosom. "Then he cried and said, 'Father Abraham, have mercy on me, and send Lazarus that he may dip the tip of his finger in water and cool my tongue; for I am tormented in

> this flame.' But Abraham said, 'Son, remember that in your lifetime you received your good things, and likewise Lazarus evil things; but now he is comforted and you are tormented. And besides all this, between us and you there is a great gulf fixed, so that those who want to pass from here to you cannot, nor can those from there pass to us.' "Then he said, 'I beg you therefore, father, that you would send him to my father's house, for I have five brothers, that he may testify to them, lest they also come to this place of torment.' Abraham said to him, 'They have Moses and the prophets; let them hear them.' And he said, 'No, father Abraham; but if one goes to them from the dead, they will repent.' But he said to him, 'If they do not hear Moses and the prophets, neither will they be persuaded though one rise from the dead.'" (Luke 16:19–31)

Those who died before Jesus Christ's resurrection either went to Hades or Paradise depending on their obedience to God's law. Jesus spoke to the criminal on the cross and said this to him: "Assuredly, I say to you, today you will be with Me in Paradise" (Luke 23:43). Paradise was a place of rest and comfort and Hades was a place of torment. When Christ died on the cross, He ascended into Hades and preached so that those there might be judged. Jesus did not preach a salvation message because it was too late for that. "For Christ also suffered once for sins, the just for the unjust, that He might bring us to God, being put to death in the flesh but made alive by the Spirit, by whom also He went and preached to the spirits in prison, who formerly were disobedient, when once the Divine longsuffering waited in the days of Noah, while the ark was being prepared, in which a few, that is, eight souls, were saved through water" (1 Peter 3:18–20). When Jesus was in Hades he retrieved the keys of Hades and death which Satan had gained in the Garden of Eden when Adam and Eve sinned. Before the fall of man, God gave Adam and Eve dominion and authority over His entire creation and they had the gift of eternal life because they had free access to the tree of life. When they sinned and rebelled against God by listening to the lies of Satan, they were exiled from the Garden. They no longer had access to the tree of life and thereby death entered into the physical bodies of Adam and Eve. The first Adam gave up the keys to life by sinning and experienced death, but the last Adam, Jesus Christ, retrieved the keys of Hades and death and was resurrected to life. By His death and resurrection, Jesus conquered death and provided eternal life to all who would believe and receive His gift. "But now Christ is risen from the dead, and has become the firstfruits of those who have fallen asleep. For since by man came death, by Man also came the resurrection of the dead. For as in Adam all die, even so in Christ all shall be made alive" (1 Corinthians 15:20–22). When Adam and Eve sinned they gave the keys of authority to Satan which became the keys of Hades and death. When Jesus descended into hell and retrieved the keys of Hades and death, He took the keys of authority away from Satan and restored them to mankind. Once these key were placed rightfully back into the hands of man, they were no longer the keys of Hades and death, but now they were the keys of the kingdom of heaven. "And I also say to you that you are Peter, and on this rock I will build My church, and the gates of Hades shall not prevail against it. And I will give you the keys of the kingdom of heaven, and whatever you bind on earth will be bound in heaven, and whatever you loose on earth will be loosed in heaven" (Matthew 16:18–19). Every born again believer possesses the keys of the kingdom of heaven, although a large portion of the church is not aware of it. Apart from blinding people about the truth of Jesus Christ, this is by far one of the greatest deceptions of Satan. He has blinded the church that they possess the keys to the kingdom of heaven and that Satan is a defeated foe. Those that belong to Jesus Christ have power over Satan and his demons because of the finished work of the cross. Jesus gave these keys of authority to the body of Christ to use according to His will so that we could establish the kingdom of heaven on earth. The keys that the Lord gave to man to operate with his restored authority, was to bind and to loose. The Greek word for "bind" is *deo* and means "to be in bonds, knit, tie, or wind." The Greek word for "loose" is *luo* which means "to break up, destroy, dissolve, melt, or put off." We have the authority to bind Satan and his demons and we have the authority to loose those captives who are under Satan's power. The Holy Spirit spoke this to me regarding binding and loosing. *"Child, all power and authority has been given to My Church to circumvent the enemy. You have My power to bind principalities, powers, rulers of darkness, and wickedness in high places. You have My power to set the captives free by loosing them from the forces of evil. This is done by the spoken word through the power of My name. If you ask anything in My name, I will do it! Just believe what you speak and it shall be done. If you say to this mountain, "Be moved" and believe it, I will move the mountain for you. Bind the rulers of darkness controlling an area so their evil influence is made ineffective. Child, dominion of the earth has been given to man. Events that occur on the earth must be approved or stopped by man. That is why it is so important to be in agreement with Me about a situation. If I am willing to permit something, and man approves it, then it will happen. If I am not willing to permit something and certain men approve it, then I call upon My people to pray to stop it. Prayers can stop such an event if My people will pray! My people need to be aware of what I am revealing and agree with Me. I will show you great and mighty things for My purposes and plans to be fulfilled. When I show you a future event and do not instruct you to pray, it will surely happen. When I show you a future event that I am opposed to, then I will instruct you to pray against it. Whatever you bind on earth will be bound in heaven and whatever you loose on earth will be loosed in heaven."* A practical application to binding would be to tie Satan's hands and his demons that are in control of a location such as a church, an area, a city, or even a nation. But this must be done through prayer by the leading of the Holy Spirit. The application of loosing pertains to people who are under the influence of Satan and his demons. People who are held captive by the enemy through alcohol, drugs, sexual addictions, sicknesses, diseases, depression and spiritual blindness need to be loosed. The power and authority to bind and loose in the name of Jesus through His shed blood is not to be used to accomplish our own selfish desires. To use the keys of the kingdom, we must be in complete harmony with the will of God. It is God's will for people to be born again by His Spirit, to be set free from sin, healed of sicknesses, set free from the pain of sorrow, and be released from all the influences of Satan. The key to using the name of Jesus is to release the authority of His name by faith through the spoken word. Here is an example how to pray using the keys of the kingdom. "In the name of Jesus Christ, I loose, I break up; I destroy and put off the spirit of drug addiction that is upon Peter. Father, draw Peter to the love of Your Son Jesus Christ. Holy Spirit, reveal to him the Truth and birth him into the kingdom of God. In the name of Jesus Christ, I speak in great faith that Peter is a mighty man of God full of His truth and His light. All chains of addiction are broken in Peter's life by the power of Jesus' name."

Jesus explained the symbolism and said that the seven stars were the seven angels of the churches and the seven golden lampstands were the seven churches. Throughout the book of Revelation when symbolism is used by either Jesus or an angel, then that symbolism is explained by them. The rest of the book of Revelation is not symbolic, but exactly what John has seen and recorded. John had been given many visions, and when he saw those things in the Spirit, he recorded them. Some of the things that he was shown he had never witnessed before, so he was not familiar with the objects or events shown to him. So he simply described the unfamiliar scenes and objects by comparing them to familiar objects that he knew. This example may help you to understand. I am in the outback of Australia and I see a wild animal in the desert and my guide tells me it is a mountain devil. I have never seen this animal before, but in a phone conversation I begin to describe this unusual looking animal. I say, "It looks like an iguana but with spiked armor. Its face looks like a rhinoceros and on the side of the face it looks like conch shells protruding. The brown leather spiked skin has the appearance of weathered walkway stones and it has claws like a turtle." By describing the unfamiliar mountain devil by using familiar animals and objects, a person can get a visual picture of this harmless desert dweller. The Apostle John employed the same method of description in the book of Revelation by using familiar things to describe unfamiliar things. The objects, events, and people that were shown to John are not symbolic; they are just as real as that mountain devil that I described. When symbolism is used in the book of Revelation, then the symbolism is explained within the text, or understood because that symbolism was used in previous Scriptures. Otherwise, the events, objects and people are real. This is important to understanding Revelation.

The seven churches that Jesus addressed were existing churches at the time period that John was writing the book of Revelation. Ephesus, Smyrna, Pergamos, Thyatira, Sardis, Philadelphia, and Laodicea all had sin that needed to be corrected in order for them to remain as a church of Jesus Christ. Jesus first pointed out the positive aspects of each church before He gave His rod of correction, and then He spoke of the reward for those who overcame and corrected the infractions. The final message that Jesus gave each church was this: "He who has an ear, let him hear what the Spirit says to the churches." The Holy Spirit opened up a great understanding to me why the Lord Jesus spoke this phrase seven times to the seven churches in Asia Minor. First and foremost, when the Lord pointed out a sin that needed to be repented of, He always revealed His solution in Scripture. This theme is repeated time and time again from Genesis to Revelation. Each of the seven churches in Asia Minor had very specific sins that needed to be dealt with and each of the seven Spirits of God had the revelation that each church needed to overcome its sin. The key to each of the seven churches' success was to "to have an ear to hear what the Spirit is saying to the churches." These seven Spirits of God identified in Isaiah have the Spirit's answer for the sin in each of the seven churches.

Spirit of the Lord
Spirit of wisdom
Spirit of understanding

Spirit of counsel
Spirit of might
Spirit of knowledge
Spirit of the fear of the Lord

The spiritual condition of each of these seven churches in Asia Minor at the time John wrote Revelation also speaks of spiritual conditions that have existed throughout the entire church age, including today. These spiritual conditions are also representative of individuals within a body of believers. The message of hope and admonition that Jesus spoke to each of the seven churches was not only pertinent then, but is also very relevant to churches today.

Revelation 2:1–7, The Church of Ephesus

> To the angel of the church of Ephesus write, 'These things says He who holds the seven stars in His right hand, who walks in the midst of the seven golden lampstands: "I know your works, your labor, your patience, and that you cannot bear those who are evil. And you have tested those who say they are apostles and are not, and have found them liars; and you have persevered and have patience, and have labored for My name's sake and have not become weary. Nevertheless I have this against you, that you have left your first love. Remember therefore from where you have fallen; repent and do the first works, or else I will come to you quickly and remove your lampstand from its place—unless you repent. But this you have, that you hate the deeds of the Nicolaitans, which I also hate. He who has an ear, let him hear what the Spirit says to the churches. To him who overcomes I will give to eat from the tree of life, which is in the midst of the Paradise of God.

Accolades: Jesus commended the church of Ephesus for laboring for His name's sake, not becoming weary, exhibiting perseverance and patience, uncovering false prophets, and hating the deeds of the Nicolaitans. The Nicolaitans were teachers in the body of Christ who began to elevate the clergy above laity. Creating ranks between clergy and laity caused divisions that destroyed holy fellowship, created strife and fostered envy. This was a great evil in God's sight and Jesus condemned the very practice of the Pharisees. The church of Ephesus was commended for their servanthood towards one another and they did not permit these false apostles to gain control by self-elevation. The Ephesians also labored with perseverance and patience to spread the gospel of Jesus Christ.

Rod of Correction: The church of Ephesus was commended for their works, but they had left their first love, Jesus Christ. How could a church with such a good track record of spreading the gospel, ministering and serving the body of Christ, and uncovering false church leaders not love Jesus? The Ephesians had replaced their intimate relationship with Jesus with good works and service, and in the process they lost their passionate love for their Lord. When the Ephesians first came into a personal relationship with Jesus, they no doubt gladly spent time in prayer, worship, and studying the Holy Scriptures because of their intense love for their Lord. Out of their great love affair with the Lord Jesus they began to labor for His name sake, which is a commendable thing. But when their works became a replacement for Him, they lost their first love. If you find yourself doing so much for the Lord that you neglect your personal time with Him, the love relationship fades on your part. Then as time goes by, that love relationship is solely based on how much work you perform for the Lord. The mindset that becomes a driving factor is the more you can do for the Lord, the more He will approve of you and love you. At this point, you have lost your ardent love for Jesus. The church of Ephesus and many churches need to be reminded never to neglect the intimate relationship with Jesus, nor to neglect the good works that God prepared in advance for them to complete. There must be balance, for out of a genuinely intense love relationship with Jesus, all good work and ministry is birthed.

Solution: Keeping Jesus as your first love can only happen by the power of the *Spirit of the Lord.* It is His Spirit that will reveal to you if your love for Jesus has diminished. Take time to listen to the Spirit of the Lord and then take action. Ask the Spirit to restore or renew your passion for Jesus. The Spirit of the Lord could be telling you right now to put this book down for now and spend some intimate time with Jesus. You may even be a minister that has dedicated your entire life to feeding His flock, but at the expense of losing your first love. The Spirit of the Lord may be whispering into your ear that Jesus is longing for a one-on-one time with you. Even as I write this book, the Spirit of the Lord is prompting me to finish this section and then retreat to my Jesus Rock. It is called my Jesus Rock because it is a large boulder in a secluded wooded area that overlooks a pond where I spend reflective time with Him. Alone with Jesus and focusing on Him and no one else, the Lord whispered in my ear these most cherished words. *"My child, I love you. Your heart is tender and pliable in My hands. You belong to Me and I will show Myself strong on your behalf. Walk with Me. Talk with Me. Dance with Me. Celebrate with Me. Sing with Me. My dear sweet Patricia, lavish your love upon Me, for I am your God, your Savior, your Light and Salvation."* When the God of this universe meets with me and talks with me, I have a sense of complete awe and my love is magnified for Him. It is at moments like these that my heart feels like it will shatter into a million pieces because I cannot possibly contain His passionate love for me. Love means everything to God, for nothing satisfies His heart as does our love. He created us to love Him for all eternity and He desires that we give our complete love and devotion to Him. He loves us with an intensity that is beyond your comprehension. Let these words of God reach the depths of your heart. *"I love you with a depth, a height, and a width that you cannot fathom. My love for you is pure and I love you like no other. I know you. I know your thoughts, your desires, your pain, your sorrow, your fears, your uncertainty, and your doubts. I know when you lie down and when you rise up. I know those things that you have kept hidden. I know the number of your days and I have numbered the hairs on your head. My love is perfect towards you because I lavish My love upon you whether you love Me in return or not. My love for you is not dependant on your love for Me; it is not a conditional love. I loved you before the beginning of time. I loved you when I formed you in your mother's womb. I loved you when you took your first breath on earth. I loved you as a child playing and frolicking. I loved you as a teenager searching for the answers to life. I loved you as a young adult entering into the service, college, the job market. I loved you when you became a spouse and when you became a parent. My eyes are always on you. I love you now with an everlasting love that is perfect and unconditional. Receive My love. Embrace My gift of love through Jesus My Son."*

Reward: Jesus promises that those who keep Him as their first love will eat from the tree of life in the Paradise of God. The tree of life provides eternal life to all who partake of it in the New Jerusalem that will come down from heaven. This is where the children of God will live forever with Jesus Christ, God the Father, and the Holy Spirit for all eternity.

Revelation 2:8–11—Church of Smyrna

> And to the angel of the church in Smyrna write, "These things says the First and the Last, who was dead, and came to life: "I know your works, tribulation, and poverty (but you are rich); and I know the blasphemy of those who say they are Jews and are not, but are a synagogue of Satan. Do not fear any of those things which you are about to suffer. Indeed, the devil is about to throw some of you into prison, that you may be tested, and you will have tribulation ten days. Be faithful until death, and I will give you the crown of life. He who has an ear, let him hear what the Spirit says to the churches. He who overcomes shall not be hurt by the second death."

Accolades: Jesus commended the church of Smyrna for their works through extreme persecution and poverty and He called them rich because of their suffering. Jesus warned them of future imprisonments and tribulations and instructed them to be faithful.

Rod of Correction: The only correction that Jesus gave this church was to fear not what they would suffer. Fear can be a paralyzing emotion that Satan uses to cause people to deny their faith in extreme circumstances. "And do not fear those who kill the body but cannot kill the soul. But rather fear Him who is able to destroy both soul and body in hell. Are not two sparrows sold for a copper coin? And not one of them falls to the ground apart from your Father's will. But the very hairs of your head are all numbered. Do not fear therefore; you are of more value than many sparrows" (Matthew 10:28–31).Up to this point in the history of the church, Christians had been crucified, burned at the stake, beheaded, imprisoned, tortured, torn apart by wild beasts, and exiled. The Christians understood from the teachings of Jesus that to deny Him, even under the penalty of death or torture, meant that they gave up their eternal life in heaven. The most powerful witness for the Lord is one that does not fear dying for the gospel. Nothing can stop that person from proclaiming His truth except physical death. That is what made Paul such a powerful Apostle—he did not fear death. Any fear that suppresses the witness of Christ or incapacitates the believer is from Satan. The fear that is prevalent in churches today is sharing the gospel message with friends, family, and neighbors. Some are afraid to openly share their faith with those close to them because they value their friend's perception of them more than they value the friend. If they truly valued and loved the friend, then nothing in heaven or on earth would stop them from proclaiming the truth about Jesus Christ. Fear of rejection is another paralyzing fear that can manipulate and devastate, especially if a person has already experienced extreme pain in this area. The Lord spoke these words to me because at times I struggle with the fear of rejection. *"Lay the fear of rejection at My feet. You will be rejected by some and embraced by others. If you let the fear of rejection be your guide, then you will miss out on opportunities that I have for you to be My witness."*

Solution: Fear of suffering, fear of death, fear of man, fear of rejection, fear of Satan, or any fears in life can resolutely be overcome by the *Spirit of the fear of the Lord.* When one has a reverential awe and fear of the

Almighty God, then all other fears are rightly put in their place. "For God has not given us a spirit of fear, but of power and of love and of a sound mind" (2 Timothy 1:7). Even if you are staring death in the face as a result of remaining steadfast in your faith in Jesus Christ, the Spirit of the fear of the Lord will divinely give you strength to give up your life if necessary. On April 20, 1999 in a small suburban town of Littleton, Colorado, two high school seniors planned a vicious assault on their peers. The seventeen-year-old girl at Columbine High School was a modern day martyr who stared death in the face but did not deny her Savior while a gun was pointed at her. She had a holy reverential love for her Lord Jesus, and in her dire time of need, the Spirit of the fear of the Lord imparted courage so she could stand up to her oppressor. She lost her life in one moment and went into the presence of her Lord the very next moment. There are also countless people that have chosen to give up their lives to serve the Lord full-time. Some have traveled to foreign lands and left family and friends behind; some have chosen to remain unmarried in order to devote their entire lives to serving the Lord; some have had spouses and family members reject them because of their Christianity; some have given up lives of monetary ease to be the Lord's vessels; and some have worked tirelessly all their lives to feed and train the sheep. "Then He said to them all, 'If anyone desires to come after Me, let him deny himself, and take up his cross daily, and follow Me. For whoever desires to save his life will lose it, but whoever loses his life for My sake will save it. For what profit is it to a man if he gains the whole world, and is himself destroyed or lost? For whoever is ashamed of Me and My words, of him the Son of Man will be ashamed when He comes in His own glory, and in His Father's, and of the holy angels'" (Luke 9:23–26).

Reward: He who loses his life for the sake of Jesus Christ will have eternal life and will be given a crown of life. Losing one's life for the sake of the gospel doesn't always mean a physical death. Losing one's life for the sake of the gospel can be laying your personal desires aside to labor for the Lord in the fullness that He has called you to serve. Those that choose to sacrifice things that are dear to them for the sake of the gospel will be given a crown of life.

Revelation 2:12–17—Church of Pergamos

> And to the angel of the church in Pergamos write, "These things says He who has the sharp two-edged sword: I know your works, and where you dwell, where Satan's throne is. And you hold fast to My name, and did not deny My faith even in the days in which Antipas was My faithful martyr, who was killed among you, where Satan dwells. But I have a few things against you, because you have there those who hold the doctrine of Balaam, who taught Balak to put a stumbling block before the children of Israel, to eat things sacrificed to idols, and to commit sexual immorality. Thus you also have those who hold the doctrine of the Nicolaitans, which thing I hate. Repent, or else I will come to you quickly and will fight against them with the sword of My mouth. He who has an ear, let him hear what the Spirit says to the churches. To him who overcomes I will give some of the hidden manna to eat. And I will give him a white stone, and on the stone a new name written which no one knows except him who receives it."

Accolades: Jesus commended the church of Pergamos for remaining strong and refusing to deny His name, even when people were being martyred among them. This was a strong church to endure the atrocities of Satan's reign without succumbing to fear.

Rod of Correction: Although Pergamos was spiritually strong, there were those within the church that held to separation of clergy and laity which is the doctrine of the Nicolaitans. The doctrine of Balaam was also prevalent in Pergamos. In the book of Numbers, Balaam was a prophet who mixed the religious practice of the heathens with those of God. When Balak, the King of Moab called upon Balaam to curse the Israelites, Balaam used sorcery as well as setting up altars to the God of Israel. Three times

Balak asked Balaam to curse Israel and three times Balaam rehearsed the words that God had given him that blessed Israel bountifully. With ever increasing riches and treasures dangled before Balaam, he finally gave Balak instructions to cause the God of Israel to curse them. He told them to let the Israelites remain in Acacia and encourage the Moabite women to marry the Israelite men. Once they committed harlotry with the women of Moab, then idolatry would be the next step that would invite the curse of God. "They invited the people to sacrifice to their gods, and the people ate and bowed down to their gods. So Israel was joined with Baal of Peor, and the anger of the Lord was aroused against Israel" (Numbers 25:2–3). The doctrine of Balaam is mixing other religious beliefs and practices with those of Christianity. Enticing Christians to form covenant relationships with unbelievers is a doctrine of Balaam. God set forth a principle of separation for the Israelites in the Old Testament and the same principle of separation for the Christians in the New Testament.

> Do not be unequally yoked together with unbelievers. For what fellowship has righteousness with lawlessness? And what communion has light with darkness? And what accord has Christ with Belial? Or what part has a believer with an unbeliever? And what agreement has the temple of God with idols? For you are the temple of the living God. As God has said:
>
> "I will dwell in them
> And walk among them.
> I will be their God,
> And they shall be My people."
>
> Therefore
>
> "Come out from among them
> And be separate, says the Lord.
> Do not touch what is unclean,
> And I will receive you."
> I will be a Father to you

> And you shall be My sons and daughters,
> Says the LORD Almighty."
> (2 Corinthians 6:14–18)

Believers should not date or marry unbelievers, should not be business partners with unbelievers, nor should believers invite unbelievers into the holy convocation of believers for Sunday worship. Nowhere in Scripture does it say that we are to invite the unsaved into our sacred and holy gathering of the saints to worship our Lord. The call from the pulpit has been to invite your lost friends to church so they can hear the gospel. The church has adopted this wrong philosophy because they have become complacent and lazy about evangelizing the lost. Inviting those that do not know Jesus Christ as Lord and Savior into your Sunday worship is like inviting an enemy into your camp. In fact, all throughout Scripture, those who rebelled against God were removed so that their poison did not spread. Ishmael was sent away because he was not the son of promise. Esau who was a fornicator that disdained and sold his holy birthright was forever cut off from God's blessing. Nadab and Abihu, the sons of Aaron, offered profane fire in the temple and a fire came out from God and killed them. Ananias and Sapphira were struck dead by God for lying to the Holy Spirit about the amount of money they gave to the church. All throughout the Word of God, rebellious people were not permitted to dwell or worship with the people of God, so why would God change His mode of operation now? The answer is that God has not changed, but the church has. The church has openly invited unbelievers into their holy gathering and expected God to bless their misguided efforts of evangelism. Scriptures warn us of such unholy actions of yoking with unbelievers because they will cause dissension, division, and discord among God's people. The church service is not the place to invite the unsaved, despite what the church is practicing. But if an unbeliever happens to come to church, he or she may be seeking the things of God and should be embraced. There is a difference between an unbeliever being led by the Holy Spirit into the house of the Lord and the open invitation to bring your unsaved friends to a Sunday service. The church can set apart a separate event for an evangelistic outreach where the only focus is to give the gospel message to the lost. In that instance, it is an evangelistic outreach and not the holy gathering of God's people to worship Him. True evangelism in the Biblical pattern happened outside the church walls and once someone was saved they were baptized and then added to the church. We gather to worship the Lord and only a born-again believer can worship God in Spirit and in truth.

Solution: The Lord Jesus was speaking to Pergamos and also to the churches today to repent of being unequally yoked with unbelievers in all aspects of their lives. This does not mean that Christians should live a monk-like life isolating themselves from unbelievers. Christians are called to be His light in a dark world by reaching the lost with the gospel. It means that we are not to make a covenant with unbelievers and the *Spirit of knowledge* will expose this wrong doctrine of joining or yoking with unbelievers. The Spirit of knowledge communicates God's answer to being only yoked with believers through the study of Scriptures, but a lack of knowledge of the Scriptures brings about destruction and death. "My people are destroyed for lack of knowledge" (Hosea 4:6). The Spirit of knowledge takes the Word of God from the pages of the Bible and writes them on the tablets of our hearts so that we can personally know God. "Then I will give them a heart to know Me, that I am the LORD; and they shall be My people, and I will be their God, for they shall return to Me with their whole heart" (Jeremiah 24:7).

Reward: The person who overcomes this errant doctrine will be given hidden manna to eat. Manna was supernaturally sent down from heaven to feed the Israelites and in the same way, the Spirit of knowledge will supernaturally feed the hungry Christian and reveal hidden manna in the Word of God. "Thus says the LORD to His anointed. I will give you the treasures of darkness and hidden riches of secret places, that you may know that I the LORD, who call you by your name, AM the God of Israel"

(Isaiah 45:1, 3). As a reward, we will be given a new name to reflect our heritage in God.

Revelation 2:18–29—Church of Thyatira

> And to the angel of the church in Thyatira write, "These things says the Son of God, who has eyes like a flame of fire, and His feet like fine brass: 'I know your works, love, service, faith, and your patience; and as for your works, the last are more than the first. Nevertheless I have a few things against you, because you allow that woman Jezebel, who calls herself a prophetess, to teach and seduce My servants to commit sexual immorality and eat things sacrificed to idols. And I gave her time to repent of her sexual immorality, and she did not repent. Indeed I will cast her into a sickbed, and those who commit adultery with her into great tribulation, unless they repent of their deeds. I will kill her children with death, and all the churches shall know that I am He who searches the minds and hearts. And I will give to each one of you according to your works. Now to you I say, and to the rest in Thyatira, as many as do not have this doctrine, who have not known the depths of Satan, as they say, I will put on you no other burden. But hold fast what you have till I come. And he who overcomes, and keeps My works until the end, to him I will give power over the nations—'He shall rule them with a rod of iron; They shall be dashed to pieces like the potter's vessels'—as I also have received from My Father; and I will give him the morning star. He who has an ear, let him hear what the Spirit says to the churches."

Accolades: Jesus commended the church of Thyatira for their love, service, faith, patience and works and He told them to hold fast to all these excellent things.

Rod of Correction: Although this church seemingly had it all together, there was a major crisis in leadership and false doctrine was being taught. This woman in the church of Thyatira was a self-appointed prophet who had the same evil influence over the body of Christ that Jezebel had over King Ahab. Ahab did more evil in the sight of God than all the previous kings before him. He married Jezebel who was from Sidonia and immediately converted to her pagan practice of Baal worship. Jezebel killed the prophets of God and set out to kill Elijah who had killed all her false prophets at Mount Carmel. Jezebel had a murderous spirit and used lies and deceit to procure for her husband the much coveted vineyard of Naboth. This teacher and seducer of the church of Thyatira used the same mode of operation as Jezebel. She had a murderous spirit that seduced the servants of the Lord by using lies and deceit to persuade them to commit sexually immoral acts. She convinced the people that these perverse sexual acts were God-given and acceptable. God's Word says that the "sexually immoral, sorcerers, idolaters, and all liars shall have their part in the lake which burns with fire and brimstone which is the second death" (Revelation 21:8). This murderous spirit operates by convincing people with lies and deception to participate in an evil activity that will be judged by God and the ultimate punishment will be the lake of fire. Churches today are being strongly warned by the Lord not to succumb to the erroneous teaching that sexual immorality of any kind is acceptable in the sight of God. Adultery, fornication, pedophilia, rape, prostitution, pornography, and homosexuality will be severely judged by God if there is no repentance. Churches that embrace homosexuality by ordaining homosexual ministers and marrying same sex couples have been seduced by the same Jezebel spirit as the church of Thyatira. Jesus pronounced the punishment of this sexual immorality would be a sickbed, great tribulation and death. We have witnessed this sickbed and death with the worldwide spread of AIDS/HIV and many incurable sexually transmitted diseases. There will be entire churches that will be cast into the lake of fire because self-appointed Jezebels convinced their congregations that homosexuality was not a sin. "You shall not lie with a male as with a woman. It is an abomination." "If a man lies with a male as he lies with a woman, both of them have committed an abomination. They shall surely be put to death. Their blood shall be upon them" (Leviticus 18:22 and 20:13). How can entire churches and denominations just ignore God's warning about homosexuality? The answer is in Scripture. They exchanged the truth of God's Word for the lie because they desired to fulfill their evil lusts without feeling guilty or being convicted of their sin.

> Therefore God also gave them up to uncleanness, in the lusts of their hearts, to dishonor their bodies among themselves, who exchanged the truth of God for the lie, and worshiped and served the creature rather than the Creator, who is blessed forever. Amen. For this reason God gave them up to vile passions. For even their women exchanged the natural use for what is against nature. Likewise also the men, leaving the natural use of the woman, burned in their lust for one another, men with men committing what is shameful, and receiving in themselves the penalty of their error which was due. And even as they did not like to retain God in their knowledge, God gave them over to a debased mind, to do those things which are not fitting; being filled with all unrighteousness, sexual immorality, wickedness, covetousness, maliciousness; full of envy, murder, strife, deceit, evil-mindedness; they are whisperers, backbiters, haters of God, violent, proud, boasters, inventors of evil things, disobedient to parents, undiscerning, untrustworthy, unloving, unforgiving, unmerciful; who, knowing the righteous judgment of God, that those who practice such things are deserving of death, not only do the same but also approve of those who practice them. (Romans 1:24–32)

Solution: *The Spirit of wisdom* will uncover all deception and expose the Jezebels that are feeding the flock with lies. Jesus is the personification of wisdom and He defines wisdom as anyone who hears God's Word and obeys. "Therefore whoever hears these sayings of Mine, and does them, I will liken him to a wise man who built his house on the rock" (Matthew 7:24). The Spirit of wisdom unveils the application of knowledge obtained through God's Word to govern your life. The key to unlocking the Spirit of wisdom is to have a direct knowledge of God's Word by reading the Bible and then obeying the commands set forth by the Lord.

Reward: For those who operate in the Spirit of wisdom by hearing and obeying God's Word, Jesus makes a phenomenal promise. Jesus will give them power over nations and they will rule and reign with Him. During the millennial reign of Christ, those who have walked in the wisdom of God and have kept His words will have a position of authority over towns, cities, and even nations.

REVELATION 3:1–6—CHURCH OF SARDIS

> And to the angel of the church in Sardis write, "These things says He who has the seven Spirits of God and the seven stars: 'I know your works, that you have a name that you are alive, but you are dead. Be watchful, and strengthen the things which remain, that are ready to die, for I have not found your works perfect before God. Remember therefore how you have received and heard; hold fast and repent. Therefore if you will not watch, I will come upon you as a thief, and you will not know what hour I will come upon you. You have a few names even in Sardis who have not defiled their garments; and they shall walk with Me in white, for they are worthy. He who overcomes shall be clothed in white garments, and I will not blot out his name from the Book of Life; but I will confess his name before My Father and before His angels. He who has an ear, let him hear what the Spirit says to the churches.'"

Accolades: There are only a select few in the church of Sardis who are worthy of praise because they have walked in righteousness.

Rod of Correction: Jesus warned this church that they had reputation of being a church that was alive in Christ, but in reality they were dead. This was a church that had a name of being a church but did nothing outside in the community. Today this would be a church where evangelism and missions are nonexistent because most of the people sitting in the pews aren't even saved. The offerings collect dust in a low interest CD that has been designated for emergency use only. Instead of sowing into the kingdom work, they are busy with raffles, spaghetti dinners, bake sales, and carnivals. The house of God has been made into a den of thieves instead of a house of prayer. "Then He went into the temple and began to drive out those who bought and sold in it, saying to them, 'It is written, "My house is a house of prayer," but you have made it a 'den of thieves'" (Luke 19:45–46). The works of this church are not pure because all works must have their foundation in Jesus Christ to be found perfect in God's sight. "For no other foundation can anyone lay than that which is laid, which is Jesus Christ. Now if anyone builds on this foundation with gold, silver, precious stones, wood, hay, straw, each one's work will become clear; for the Day will declare it, because it will be revealed by fire; and the fire will test each one's work, of what sort it is. If anyone's work which he has built on it endures, he will receive a reward. If anyone's work is burned, he will suffer loss; but he himself will be saved, yet so as through fire" (1 Corinthians 3:11–15). Jesus Christ must be the central person of worship in order for a church to keep its candle burning and remain a church. There can be no other person or object that is worshipped alongside Jesus.

Solution: The church of Sardis had a lack of understanding what it meant to be a true church of Jesus Christ. This dead church needed *The Spirit of understanding* breathed upon them to miraculously transform them. They needed to recognize that salvation comes through Jesus Christ alone by His death on the cross and resurrection from the dead. An individual must personally ask Jesus to forgive his sins and to be his Lord and Savior. Salvation begins by acknowledging that you are a sinner that deserves to be punished. Confessing your sins to Jesus with a repentant heart and believing with your heart that Jesus Christ took your punishment on the cross is paramount to receiving His gift of salvation. Acknowledging that Jesus rose from the dead on the third day and is seated at the right hand of the Father is a tenant of faith that must be believed and professed. Salvation is not an intellectual knowledge about Jesus. Salvation is not attending church every Sunday. Salvation is not about being a good person, a generous person, or even a loving person. Salvation through Jesus Christ is not a hope, it is a fact. When you ask Jesus Christ to forgive your sins and be your Savior, your sins are forgiven and you have eternal life in heaven! There's no hoping that you will make it to heaven; you absolutely know! Believing, receiving, loving and obeying Jesus Christ as your Lord and Savior is salvation!

Reward: Those who have been born again by receiving salvation through Jesus Christ will be given white robes; their names will be written in the Book of Life; and Jesus will confess their names before God the Father and His angels. They will have a place in heaven for all eternity where all pain, sorrow, and sickness have been wiped away and replaced with joy, peace, and divine health embodied in glorified bodies.

REVELATION 3:7–13—CHURCH OF PHILADELPHIA

> And to the angel of the church in Philadelphia write, "These things says He who is holy, He who is true, 'He who has the key of David, He who opens and no one shuts, and shuts and no one opens': I know your works. See, I have set before you an open door, and no one can shut it; for you have a little strength, have kept My word, and have not denied My name. Indeed I will make those of the synagogue of Satan, who say they are Jews and are not, but lie—indeed I will make them come and worship before your feet, and to know that I have loved you. Because you have kept My command to persevere, I also will keep you from the hour of trial which shall come upon the whole world, to test those who dwell on the earth. Behold, I am coming quickly! Hold fast what you have, that no one may take your crown. He who overcomes, I will

> make him a pillar in the temple of My God, and he shall go out no more. I will write on him the name of My God and the name of the city of My God, the New Jerusalem, which comes down out of heaven from My God. And I will write on him My new name. "He who has an ear, let him hear what the Spirit says to the churches."

Accolades: The church of Philadelphia was commended for keeping the commands of the Word of God, for persevering and not denying the name of Christ. This church made the Word of God their final authority in all aspects of their lives. They did not compromise His Word by omitting passages that did not fit their lifestyle or were not relevant to their culture or time. Instead, they kept the Lord's command to persevere.

Rod of Correction: This nearly perfect church only lacked in one area and that was uncovered when Jesus told them they only had a little strength. It may seem like a small thing, but if their spiritual strength continued to dwindle, they would not be able to hold fast to obeying God's Word. There are some churches today that have dwindled in spiritual strength and have not held fast to the Word of God because they choose what parts of the Bible they will obey. These are some biblical truths that a spiritually weak church will not observe, and those are tithing, regular church attendance, water baptism following salvation, and the operation of spiritual gifts within the body of believers. This kind of church lacks spiritual power because disobedience to these biblical truths has robbed them of spiritual growth and blessings. God said that those that obey His truths will be blessed. Jesus spoke more on the subject of giving than any other subject because He knew that is was not in the hearts of men to give, especially to God.

> "Bring all the tithes into the storehouse,
> That there may be food in My house,
> And try Me now in this,"

> Says the LORD of hosts,
> "If I will not open for you the windows of heaven
> And pour out for you such blessing
> That there will not be room enough to receive it."
> (Malachi 3:10)

Tithing is a subject that pastors are the most uncomfortable preaching about because people do not want to hear that God requires them to give back to Him one tenth of all that He has given them. Tithing is an act of obedience and an act of faith. It becomes an act of faith when you take the one tenth part and give it to God believing that He will continue to supply for you, especially when you need that one tenth to pay the bills. Tithing is giving God the first portion, the best portion, the cream off the top. I remember as a child when my parents would go to a dairy farm and get milk in a large metal milk can and bring it home. The milk was not homogenized or pasteurized and the heavy cream would float to the top of the container. You could scoop the cream off the top and eat it before the milk was shaken up. This cream is a picture of the tithe that we are to give to the Lord. It is the choicest, the best part of the milk that the Lord deserves because He is the Giver of all the milk. Obedience to the entire Word of God will result in blessings, but disobedience results in loss. Contrary to what some churches practice, God's children do not get to choose what Biblical truths we will observe. Jesus was warning the church of Philadelphia and churches today that they need to maintain spiritual strength by obeying the entire Word of God.

Solution: Those who are weak and have diminishing spiritual power need to call upon *The Spirit of might* who will renew their strength. Their strength will be renewed by waiting upon the Lord and acting in obedience to the written Word of God. "But those who wait on the LORD shall renew their strength; they shall mount up with wings like eagles, they shall run and not be weary, they shall walk and not faint" (Isaiah 40:31). When we are weak, God's strength abounds through the Spirit of might "And He said to me, 'My grace is sufficient for you, for My strength is made perfect in weakness.' Therefore most gladly I will rather boast in my infirmities, that the power of Christ may rest upon me" (2 Corinthians 12:9).

Reward: Those who obey the whole Word of God will be pillars in the church as well as pillars in the New Jerusalem that comes down from Heaven. Jesus will write on him a new name, one that reflects his heritage and position in God. Those who keep the Lord's commands will not have to endure the hour of trial that will come upon the world during the second half of the Tribulation.

Revelation 3:14–22—Church of Laodicea

> And to the angel of the church of the Laodiceans write, "These things says the Amen, the Faithful and True Witness, the Beginning of the creation of God: I know your works, that you are neither cold nor hot. I could wish you were cold or hot. So then, because you are lukewarm, and neither cold nor hot, I will vomit you out of My mouth. Because you say, 'I am rich, have become wealthy, and have need of nothing'—and do not know that you are wretched, miserable, poor, blind, and naked— I counsel you to buy from Me gold refined in the fire, that you may be rich; and white garments, that you may be clothed, that the shame of your nakedness may not be revealed; and anoint your eyes with eye salve, that you may see. As many as I love, I rebuke and chasten. Therefore be zealous and repent. Behold, I stand at the door and knock. If anyone hears My voice and opens the door, I will come in to him and dine with him, and he with Me. To him who overcomes I will grant to sit with Me on My throne, as I also overcame and sat down with My Father on His throne. He who has an ear, let him hear what the Spirit says to the churches."

Accolades: Jesus had absolutely no praise for this lukewarm church.

Rod of Correction: The rod of correction for the Laodicean church was severe. This church had one foot in the world and one foot in the church and they had become lazy and complacent. Jesus was ready to vomit this church out of His mouth which was a very severe rebuke. The Lord gave me His message regarding churches that are like the Laodicean Church. I live near a golf course and frequently take walks on this beautiful course. There are several ponds on the golf course and also a large overflow pond that the other ponds flow into during the rainy season. I was taking my usual walk when I came to this large overflow pond and was shocked to see that it was empty. All that remained of this body of water were two shallow pools of water and a lot of stagnant slimy masses of dead plant life. The smell of decaying fish and rotting plants wafted up to my nose as I stood on the edge of what used to be the bank. Very clearly I heard the Holy Spirit speak to me this about the lukewarm church. "*Stagnant! The majority of My church is stagnant. My church has bought into the ways of the world. They don't respect the sanctity of life and they turn their heads away from the abortions that are occurring. My church doesn't understand that abortion is murder and those that do understand choose to do nothing. They think that abortion is just another political issue to be debated. My covenant of marriage is not honored and when trouble arises in a marriage, the first course of action is divorce. Marriage is entered into lightly without understanding that it is a covenant that is not to be broken. Homosexuality is an accepted way of life, but it is an abomination to Me. Those that know that homosexuality is a sin refuse to speak against it because of fear. The majority of My church is stagnant, just like the empty pond you see. There is a small amount of life in the lukewarm church just as there is in those two shallow pools of water. I have a remnant of people in this church that has life and has not bought into the ways of the world*" These are harsh words that the Lord has spoken regarding the lukewarm church, but unless there is repentance, He will vomit these people out.

Solution: Jesus very clearly gave this church His answer to their sin when He said: "I counsel you to buy from Me gold refined in the fire." *The Spirit of counsel* has the precious gold for those who are in dire need of rising above mediocrity and coming out from among the practices of the world. The world says grab everything you can by whatever means it takes and do it with gusto because you only go around once. Jesus said: "But when you do a charitable deed, do not let your left hand know what your right hand is doing, that your charitable deed may be in secret; and your Father who sees in secret will Himself reward you openly" (Matthew 6:3–4). The world says look out for number one, because if you don't, no one else will, but Jesus said: "Do not lay up for yourselves treasures on earth, where moth and rust destroy and where thieves break in and steal; but lay up for yourselves treasures in heaven, where neither moth nor rust destroys and where thieves do not break in and steal. For where your treasure is, there your heart will be also" (Matthew 6:19–21). The world says you deserve the best, and if you cannot afford the best, sue your neighbor for it, but Jesus said: "If anyone wants to sue you and take away your tunic, let him have your cloak also" (Matthew 5:40). The world says that you have rights and nobody ought to violate them, but Jesus said, "Love your enemies, bless those who curse you, do good to those who hate you, and pray for those who spitefully use you and persecute you" (Matthew 5:44). Embracing the ways of the world alongside the ways of God could cost you dearly. When some stand before God, they will be surprised at what they hear and will hang their heads in shame. "Not everyone who says to Me, 'Lord, Lord,' shall enter the kingdom of heaven, but he who does the will of My Father in heaven. Many will say to Me in that day, 'Lord, Lord, have we not prophesied in Your name, cast out demons in Your name, and done many wonders in Your name?' And then I will declare to them, 'I never knew you; depart from Me, you who practice lawlessness!'" (Matthew 7:21–23).

Reward: To those who pledge themselves to the excellence of fully committing to Christ through the whole counsel of God by refusing to partake of the ways of the world, Jesus will grant them to sit with Him on His throne. "For I have not shunned to declare to you the whole counsel of God" (Acts 20:27).

Chapter Two

Behold the King

Revelation 4:1–5

After these things I looked, and behold, a door standing open in heaven. And the first voice which I heard was like a trumpet speaking with me, saying, "Come up here, and I will show you things which must take place after this." Immediately I was in the Spirit; and behold, a throne set in heaven, and One sat on the throne. And He who sat there was like a jasper and a sardius stone in appearance; and there was a rainbow around the throne, in appearance like an emerald. Around the throne were twenty-four thrones, and on the thrones I saw twenty-four elders sitting, clothed in white robes; and they had crowns of gold on their heads. And from the throne proceeded lightnings, thunderings, and voices. Seven lamps of fire were burning before the throne, which are the seven Spirits of God.

John saw a door standing open in heaven and the invitation to walk through the door was extended. For a split second John may have replayed in his mind the time when Jesus intimately spoke these words. "Most assuredly, I say to you, I am the door of the sheep. All who ever came before Me are thieves and robbers, but the sheep did not hear them. I am the door. If anyone enters by Me, he will be saved and will go in and out and find pasture (John 10:7–9). Hearing the voice of his Shepherd and responding to the Lord's invitation, John was immediately taken up to heaven to view spectacular things he would record for generations to come. The Apostle Paul was also taken up to heaven to be shown awesome things so he could gain great understanding to become an apostle to the Gentiles. God is still in the business of revealing heavenly things to His people to equip them, empower them, and prepare them to usher His kingdom to this earth. Listen to the voice of the Good Shepherd and respond to His invitation. Be fully surrendered to His will so that heavenly doors are opened and the God of this universe will reveal Himself and His plans.

While in heaven, John saw twenty-four thrones positioned around the throne of God with elders on each of these thrones. Scripture does not specifically identify these elders, but from their position around the throne of God they are of great prominence. The twelve apostles and elders from the twelve tribes of Israel certainly reflect this notable distinction. Since John was an apostle and he was taken to heaven in the Spirit, one has to ponder if he saw himself on one of those thrones. God certainly has a way of revealing future events to His children to encourage them so they can endure the hardships that will come as a result of being fully dedicated to the Lord.

John used the comparison method to describe the Lord sitting on His throne. He took familiar objects to describe this unfamiliar scene before him. He described the Lord as a jasper stone which is bright red or yellow quartz and sardius stone which is a ruby or garnet. Red and yellow are the color of flames, and three times in the book of Revelation Jesus was described as having eyes like a flame of fire. John also described a rainbow of color radiating from the throne of God. The sun's light is a white light and when it is refracted though the droplets of water in the atmosphere, the color of the rainbow can be seen by the human eye. The Son's light is a brilliant white light and when His glory was reflected through His power, a beautiful rainbow of color was displayed to John. It is so amazing how God's creation reflects His very nature and essence!

REVELATION 4:6–11

Before the throne there was a sea of glass, like crystal. And in the midst of the throne, and around the throne, were four living creatures full of eyes in front and in back. The first living creature was like a lion, the second living creature like a calf, the third living creature had a face like a man, and the fourth living creature was like a flying eagle. The four living creatures, each having six wings, were full of eyes around and within. And they do not rest day or night, saying:

"Holy, holy, holy,
Lord God Almighty,
Who was and is and is to come!"

Whenever the living creatures give glory and honor and thanks to Him who sits on the throne, who lives forever and ever, the twenty-four elders fall down before Him who sits on the throne and worship Him who lives forever and ever, and cast their crowns before the throne, saying:

"You are worthy, O Lord,
To receive glory and honor and power;
For You created all things,
And by Your will they exist and were created."

John witnessed four angelic beings that had a very unique appearance and a very exceptional task. These six winged angelic beings were seraphim that give glory, honor, and thanks to Jesus day and night by saying: "Holy, holy, holy, Lord God Almighty, Who was and is and is to come!" While Ezekiel was among the captives in Babylon, he was permitted to view cherubim when God opened up the heavens.

Then I looked, and behold, a whirlwind was coming out of the north, a great cloud with raging fire engulfing itself; and brightness

> was all around it and radiating out of its midst like the color of amber, out of the midst of the fire. Also from within it came the likeness of four living creatures. And this was their appearance: they had the likeness of a man. Each one had four faces, and each one had four wings. Their legs were straight, and the soles of their feet were like the soles of calves' feet. They sparkled like the color of burnished bronze. The hands of a man were under their wings on their four sides; and each of the four had faces and wings. Their wings touched one another. The creatures did not turn when they went, but each one went straight forward. As for the likeness of their faces, each had the face of a man; each of the four had the face of a lion on the right side, each of the four had the face of an ox on the left side, and each of the four had the face of an eagle. Thus were their faces. Their wings stretched upward; two wings of each one touched one another, and two covered their bodies.'" (Ezekiel 1:4–11)

The description of these living creatures by Ezekiel was more detailed than John's, but they are similar. The fact that Ezekiel viewed them from various angles is evident because he was able to see each of the four faces. It is apparent that John only saw these living creatures from one direction and that is why he described them as only having one face, but each with a different face. The living creatures that Ezekiel described are similar to what John described because they had the face of a lion, the face of an ox, the face of a man, and the face of an eagle. Each of the faces signified an authority over different realms. The lion is the king of the beasts, the ox is the king of domestic animals, man is king of creation, and the eagle is the king of birds. It can also be said that the lion embodies royalty because Jesus is called the Lion of the Tribe of Judah. The ox stands for sacrifice because the Israelites were instructed by God to make animal sacrifices for sin atonement. The man exemplifies intelligence and dominion over the earth that God gave to Adam and Eve in Genesis. The eagle characterizes heavenliness, as spoken by Isaiah, "But those who wait on the LORD shall renew their strength; they shall mount up with wings like eagles, they shall run and not be weary, they shall walk and not faint" (Isaiah 4:31). John saw that the seraphim had six wings and Ezekiel saw the cherubim having four wings. These six-winged and four-winged living creatures that John saw around the throne and Ezekiel saw by the Chebar River were both angelic beings with a specific purpose. The prophet Isaiah was also given a vision of unique living creatures and he identified them as seraphim. "In the year that King Uzziah died, I saw the Lord sitting on a throne, high and lifted up, and the train of His robe filled the temple. Above it stood seraphim; each one had six wings: with two he covered his face, with two he covered his feet, and with two he flew. And one cried to another and said: "Holy, holy, holy is the LORD of hosts; the whole earth is full of His glory!" (Isaiah 6:1–3). These living creatures are angelic beings whose entire purpose is to glorify God around His throne.

REVELATION 5:1–7

> And I saw in the right hand of Him who sat on the throne a scroll written inside and on the back, sealed with seven seals. Then I saw a strong angel proclaiming with a loud voice, "Who is worthy to open the scroll and to loose its seals?" And no one in heaven or on the earth or under the earth was able to open the scroll, or to look at it. So I wept much, because no one was found worthy to open and read the scroll, or to look at it. But one of the elders said to me, "Do not weep. Behold, the Lion of the tribe of Judah, the Root of David, has prevailed to open the scroll and to loose its seven seals." And I looked, and behold, in the midst of the throne and of the four living creatures, and in the midst of the elders, stood a Lamb as though it had been slain, having seven horns and seven eyes, which are the seven Spirits of God sent out into all the earth. Then He came and took the scroll out of the right hand of Him who sat on the throne.

Absorbing the scene that was unfolding in the throne room in heaven, John observed the right hand of God holding a scroll. No one has ever been permitted to see the face of God the Father except Jesus Christ, and while in heaven, John is only allowed to view His right hand. Moses was not permitted to see the face of God and this explanation was given. "But He said, 'You cannot see My face; for no man shall see Me, and live.' And the LORD said, 'Here is a place by Me, and you shall stand on the rock. So it shall be, while My glory passes by, that I will put you in the cleft of the rock, and will cover you with My hand while I pass by. Then I will take away My hand, and you shall see My back; but My face shall not be seen'" (Exodus 33:20–23). God the Father was holding a scroll with seven seals and Jesus Christ was the only one worthy to open it. Jesus was described as the Lion of the tribe of Judah, the Root of David, and a Lamb. Although the latter two were used to describe Jesus throughout the Scriptures, this is the only place that Jesus is called the Lion from the tribe of Judah. Jesus took the scroll out of the right hand of God and was prepared to step into His role as the Lion, for He had already fulfilled His role as the Lamb.

REVELATION 5:8–14

> Now when He had taken the scroll, the four living creatures and the twenty-four elders fell down before the Lamb, each having a harp, and golden bowls full of incense, which are the prayers of the saints. And they sang a new song, saying:
>
> "You are worthy to take the scroll,
> And to open its seals;
> For You were slain,
> And have redeemed us to God by Your blood
> Out of every tribe and tongue and people and nation,
> And have made us kings and priests to our God;
> And we shall reign on the earth."
>
> Then I looked, and I heard the voice of many angels around the throne, the living creatures, and the elders; and the number

> of them was ten thousand times ten thousand, and thousands of thousands, saying with a loud voice:
>
> "Worthy is the Lamb who was slain
> To receive power and riches and wisdom,
> And strength and honor and glory and blessing!"
>
> And every creature which is in heaven and on the earth and under the earth and such as are in the sea, and all that are in them, I heard saying:
>
> "Blessing and honor and glory and power
> Be to Him who sits on the throne,
> And to the Lamb, forever and ever!"
>
> Then the four living creatures said, "Amen!" And the twenty-four elders fell down and worshipped Him who lives for ever and ever."

When Jesus had taken the scroll from the Father's hand, the four seraphim and the twenty-four elders fell down and worshiped Jesus. They also had harps and golden bowls full of incense which are prayers of the saints. "Then another angel, having a golden censer, came and stood at the altar. He was given much incense, that he should offer it with the prayers of all the saints upon the golden altar which was before the throne. And the smoke of the incense, with the prayers of the saints, ascended before God from the angel's hand. Then the angel took the censer, filled it with fire from the altar, and threw it to the earth. And there were noises, thunderings, lightnings, and an earthquake" (Revelation 8:3–5). This beautiful description is a remarkable picture of how our prayers ascend to heaven and are collected in golden bowls. When the prayer bowls are full, they are mixed with incense and the prayers rise to the throne of God as a sweet aroma. God responds to that sweet aroma by answering those prayers and then He sends forth an angel with the answer to earth. An awe inspiring example of this is praying for a loved one's salvation. Sometimes years may go by as we offer up prayers for this loved one's salvation, but it seems to no avail. He or she continues to deny Christ and persists in walking in a shameful way of life. Prayers that are offered for that individual fill up the golden bowl in heaven and then God's answer comes forth. It may seem that they unexpectedly accept Christ, but much has happened in the spiritual realm as the result of our prayers that we do not see or understand. Just because we do not see the spiritual battle being waged for this one's soul does not mean it is not occurring. Daniel had prayed and fasted to gain understanding of when the exiles in Babylon would return to Israel, but there was a spiritual battle that was waged for three weeks before the angel could bring God's answer.

> Do not fear, Daniel, for from the first day that you set your heart to understand, and to humble yourself before your God, your words were heard; and I have come because of your words. But the prince of the kingdom of Persia withstood me twenty-one days; and behold, Michael, one of the chief princes, came to help me, for I had been left alone there with the kings of Persia. Now I have come to make you understand what will happen to your people in the latter days, for the vision refers to many days yet to come. (Daniel 10:12–14)

Do not ever give up praying for someone's salvation, because your prayers are accumulating in heaven and there is a spiritual battle being waged for that one's soul. Your Father in Heaven hears your prayers! You never know when that last prayer will tip the balance and God will send forth His answer by the power and the fire of the Holy Spirit. The Father is the only One who can draw people to His Son Jesus Christ and the Holy Spirit is the only One who can reveal the truth about Jesus. Be persistent before God and pray without ceasing until you get the answer for the salvation of your loved one.

The new song that was sung in heaven is one of salvation and redemption; one that every born-again Christian should be resounding here on earth. Through the shed blood of Jesus Christ on the cross, we have been redeemed and saved from the pit of hell. Not only have we traded in Satan as our father and sin as our motivator, but also we now have God as our Father and righteousness as our covering. We are joint heirs with Jesus Christ and He has transformed us from poor, wretched, hell-bound beggars to rich, joyful heaven-bound priests and kings. This redemption and transformation was guaranteed to us through Isaiah when he described the complete promises of salvation through the suffering of Jesus Christ.

> Surely He has borne our griefs
> And carried our sorrows;
> Yet we esteemed Him stricken,
> Smitten by God, and afflicted.
> But He was wounded for our transgressions,
> He was bruised for our iniquities;
> The chastisement for our peace was upon Him,
> And by His stripes we are healed.
> (Isaiah 53:4–5)

This salvation message is the complete gospel of Jesus Christ, but so many Christians receive only a partial gospel. According to this Scripture, Jesus Christ died for our physical sicknesses so that our bodies could receive divine healing. Every disease and sickness that was past, present and future was heaped upon His body so that we could call upon His name for divine healing. There is power in His name and power in His blood. When that truth goes from intellectual knowledge to a spiritual understanding then faith is released for Jesus to heal. Jesus also died so that He could deliver us from any emotional pain that has been afflicted upon us from others. Many people carry around bitterness because of the cruel actions of others or malicious words. God never meant for us to live our lives strangled by emotional pain inflicted by others, and He provided a way for us to be truly set free from that pain. It is called forgiveness. It is your forgiveness for your offender. Forgiveness does not mean that you have to trust that person again or even be friends with your offender. Forgiveness means that you no longer hold that person accountable for what he or she has done to you. Your forgiveness releases Jesus to heal your heart so that the emotional pain is divinely removed. Everything that God does is divine, so why should we be surprised that He removes our emotional pain through divine methods. There is great freedom in forgiving and there is even greater freedom in being forgiven. When Jesus hung on that cross with His body badly beaten, the nails ripping into His flesh, the thirst overwhelming, and the pain excruciating, He said: "Father, forgive them, for they do not know what they do" (Luke 23:34). Jesus also died on the cross for our iniquities or self-will. God never took away man's free will, but it is His desire for our wills to be conformed to His will. This promise of the gospel requires us to be obedient to the known will of God revealed in Scripture. When we obey the commands of God written in the Word, it prompts God to make His will known for the believer's life. God's will for the believer is not a mystery.

> For this commandment which I command you today is not too mysterious for you, nor is it far off. It is not in heaven, that you should say, "Who will ascend into heaven for us and bring it to us, that we may hear it and do it?" Nor is it beyond the sea, that you should say, "Who will go over the sea for us and bring it to us, that we may hear it and do it?" But the word is very near you, in your mouth and in your heart, that you may do it.
>
> See, I have set before you today life and good, death and evil, in that I command you today to love the LORD your God, to walk in His ways, and to keep His commandments, His statutes, and His judgments, that you may live and multiply; and the LORD your God will bless you in the land which you go to possess. (Deuteronomy 30:11–16)

So often Christians complain that they do not know what God's plans are for them while they continually disobey what is written in Scripture. If you refuse to submit to God's known will by disobeying His commands, then how do you expect God to reveal to you the weightier matters of His will and plan for your life? Be faithful in obeying God's written Word and He will be faithful to reveal His specific plans for your life. The full gospel of Jesus Christ says that He was also chastised for our peace. There are two kinds of peace: peace with God and the peace of God. Peace with God occurs the moment that we receive Jesus as Lord and Savior and our sins have been forgiven. Our relationship with God the Father has been restored because of Jesus Christ's death on the cross. The peace of God is that inner peace we can have even when our outward circumstances are in total chaos. God fills us with His peace and whispers in our ears that He is in control and that everything will be all right. This peace is supernatural because it defies all human reason and logic, but nonetheless, it is a peace felt deeply within one's soul. Jesus was wounded for our transgressions and He became the sacrificial Lamb that the Father required for the removal of our sins. Jesus came to deliver us from our sin and also to set the captives free from all that Satan has bound us with. Many people have the chains of addiction wrapped so tightly about them that they have no hope of breaking free. Drug addiction, alcoholism, sexual addictions, gluttony, and all other addictions have already been conquered at the cross. Satan your enemy just does not want you know that. By the power of the blood of the Lamb these chains are loosed and will not exercise control over you if you are willing to release them to Jesus. For a born-again Christian, an addiction only remains an addiction if you are not willing to turn from it and give it to Jesus. Jesus Christ died so you could be set free from the bondage of sin and the choice is yours whether or not you partake of that promise. Many born-again Christians do not partake of the full gospel message of deliverance, healing, and peace because of a lack of knowledge, but some out of willful disobedience. The Lamb was slain so that our sins are forgiven, bondages are broken, bodies are made well, pains and sorrows are removed, wills are conformed, and peace is abundant. The Lamb is worthy to receive glory and honor and praise!

Chapter Three

Tribulation and Rapture

Revelation 6:1–2

"Now I saw when the Lamb opened one of the seals; and I heard one of the four living creatures saying with a voice like thunder, "Come and see." And I looked, and behold, a white horse. He who sat on it had a bow; and a crown was given to him, and he went out conquering and to conquer."

Jesus took the scroll containing the seven seals from God the Father and He began to open each seal. Each of the first four seals pertains to the Antichrist as he progresses through the first three-and-a-half years of the Tribulation. In the first seal, the Antichrist is seen on a white horse showing that initially he comes in peace. He had a bow without arrows depicting that he will win the favor of people and nations with flattery, charisma, and the ability to negotiate a peace treaty with Israel and the Middle Eastern nations. But in the middle of the seven years, the Antichrist will break the peace treaty.

Then he shall confirm a covenant with many for one week;
But in the middle of the week
He shall bring an end to sacrifice and offering.
And on the wing of abominations shall be one who makes desolate,

> Even until the consummation, which is determined,
> Is poured out on the desolate.
> (Daniel 9:27)

Isaiah also prophesied about the Antichrist breaking his covenant with Israel.

> Surely their valiant ones shall cry outside,
> The ambassadors of peace shall weep bitterly.
> The highways lie waste,
> The traveling man ceases.
> He has broken the covenant,
> He has despised the cities,
> He regards no man.
> (Isaiah 33:7–8)

Revelation 6:3–4

> "When He opened the second seal, I heard the second living creature saying, 'Come and see.' Another horse, fiery red, went out. And it was granted to the one who sat on it to take peace from the earth, and that people should kill one another; and there was given to him a great sword."

In the second seal that Christ opened, the Antichrist was seen sitting on a red horse which denotes war. He will take nations by force and now the Antichrist is seen with a great sword instead of a bow without arrows.

> He shall also enter the Glorious Land, and many countries shall be overthrown; but these shall escape from his hand: Edom, Moab, and the prominent people of Ammon. He shall stretch out his hand against the countries, and the land of Egypt shall not escape. He shall have power over the treasures of gold and silver,

> and over all the precious things of Egypt; also the Libyans and Ethiopians shall follow at his heels. But news from the east and the north shall trouble him; therefore he shall go out with great fury to destroy and annihilate many. (Daniel 11:41–44)

Revelation 6:5–6

> "When He opened the third seal, I heard the third living creature say, 'Come and see.' So I looked, and behold, a black horse, and he who sat on it had a pair of scales in his hand. And I heard a voice in the midst of the four living creatures saying, 'A quart of wheat for a denarius, and three quarts of barley for a denarius; and do not harm the oil and the wine.'"

In the third seal that was opened, the Antichrist was seen sitting on a black horse with a pair of scales in his hand. The black horse is indicative of famine and the scarcity of food is noted by the purchase of one quart of wheat for one day's wage. The mention of not harming the oil and wine shows that some will live in luxury during this time of famine. It will be during this time that the false prophet will require people to take the mark of the Beast in order to buy or sell any merchandise. "He causes all, both small and great, rich and poor, free and slave, to receive a mark on their right hand or on their foreheads, and that no one may buy or sell except one who has the mark or the name of the beast, or the number of his name" (Revelation 13:16–17).

Revelation 6:7–8

> "When He opened the fourth seal, I heard the voice of the fourth living creature saying, 'Come and see.' So I looked, and behold, a pale horse. And the name of him who sat on it was Death, and Hades followed with him. And power was given to them over a fourth of the earth, to kill with sword, with hunger, with death, and by the beasts of the earth."

The fourth seal that was opened by Jesus Christ shows the Antichrist and Satan on a pale horse. At this point in the Antichrist's career, Satan has entered him and has complete control. The destruction of the earth by the sword, by hunger, and by beasts depicts the complete depravity and the darkest time of the history of mankind. Satan knows that his time is short and he will take as many people with him to hell as he possibly can. Satan's strategy has not changed in two thousand years. He employed Judas Iscariot to carry out his plans to try and destroy the Messiah and he will employ the Antichrist to rise up against Christ and His people. His wanton fury will motivate him to eradicate the Jews and the Christians. This time in history will far outweigh the atrocities of the Holocaust, the violence of any known war, or any brutality that has been perpetrated upon man.

REVELATION 6:9–11

> When He opened the fifth seal, I saw under the altar the souls of those who had been slain for the word of God and for the testimony which they held. And they cried with a loud voice, saying, "How long, O Lord, holy and true, until You judge and avenge our blood on those who dwell on the earth?" Then a white robe was given to each of them; and it was said to them that they should rest a little while longer, until both the number of their fellow servants and their brethren, who would be killed as they were, was completed.

When the fifth seal was opened by the Lord Jesus, the martyrs cried out to Him to judge and avenge their blood. Their innocent blood will be avenged, but they were instructed to rest a little longer until the full number of martyrs was complete. The number of martyrs will reach its fullness during this fifth seal when the Antichrist hunts down and violently murders the Christians. The first shedding of innocent blood was recorded in Genesis and his blood cried out for revenge also.

> Then the LORD said to Cain, "Where is Abel your brother?" He

> said, "I do not know. Am I my brother's keeper?" And He said, "What have you done? The voice of your brother's blood cries out to Me from the ground. So now you are cursed from the earth, which has opened its mouth to receive your brother's blood from your hand. When you till the ground, it shall no longer yield its strength to you. A fugitive and a vagabond you shall be on the earth." (Genesis 4:9–12)

God is a holy God and He will judge individuals as well as nations for murdering the innocent.

REVELATION 6:12–17

> I looked when He opened the sixth seal, and behold, there was a great earthquake; and the sun became black as sackcloth of hair, and the moon became like blood. And the stars of heaven fell to the earth, as a fig tree drops its late figs when it is shaken by a mighty wind. Then the sky receded as a scroll when it is rolled up, and every mountain and island was moved out of its place. And the kings of the earth, the great men, the rich men, the commanders, the mighty men, every slave and every free man, hid themselves in the caves and in the rocks of the mountains, and said to the mountains and rocks, "Fall on us and hide us from the face of Him who sits on the throne and from the wrath of the Lamb! For the great day of His wrath has come, and who is able to stand?"

It is during the sixth seal that the sky rolls back like a scroll and Jesus Christ appears in the sky and His church is caught up to Heaven. The Latin word that means "to seize, snatch, to carry off" is *raptus* and that is how the church coined the phrase–,"The Rapture of the Church." There are those that hold to the doctrine that the church will be taken up right before the beginning of the seven-year Tribulation, but many Scriptures paint a different picture. Scriptures are very clear that immediately after a time of tribulation, Jesus will appear in the sky and gather His elect. The sixth seal is definitely Christ appearing in the sky to catch up His church. This event is not to be confused with the Second coming of Christ when He places His feet upon the Mount of Olives and returns to earth. Read each of these next Scriptures and allow the Holy Spirit to reveal to you the sequence of events that unfolds and leads up to the Rapture of the Church.

> Therefore when you see the 'abomination of desolation,' spoken of by Daniel the prophet, standing in the holy place (whoever reads, let him understand), then let those who are in Judea flee to the mountains. Let him who is on the housetop not go down to take anything out of his house. And let him who is in the field not go back to get his clothes. But woe to those who are pregnant and to those who are nursing babies in those days! And pray that your flight may not be in winter or on the Sabbath. For then there will be great tribulation, such as has not been since the beginning of the world until this time, no, nor ever shall be. And unless those days were shortened, no flesh would be saved; but for the elect's sake those days will be shortened. Then if anyone says to you, "Look, here is the Christ!" or "There!" do not believe it. For false christs and false prophets will rise and show great signs and wonders to deceive, if possible, even the elect. See, I have told you beforehand. Therefore if they say to you, "Look, He is in the desert!" do not go out; or "Look, He is in the inner rooms!" do not believe it. For as the lightning comes from the east and flashes to the west, so also will the coming of the Son of Man be. For wherever the carcass is, there the eagles will be gathered together. Immediately after the tribulation of those days the sun will be darkened, and the moon will not give its light; the stars will fall from heaven, and the powers of the heavens will be shaken. Then the sign of the Son of Man will appear in heaven, and then all the

tribes of the earth will mourn, and they will see the Son of Man coming on the clouds of heaven with power and great glory. And He will send His angels with a great sound of a trumpet, and they will gather together His elect from the four winds, from one end of heaven to the other. (Matthew 24:15–31)

But in those days, after that tribulation, the sun will be darkened, and the moon will not give its light; the stars of heaven will fall, and the powers in the heavens will be shaken. Then they will see the Son of Man coming in the clouds with great power and glory. And then He will send His angels, and gather together His elect from the four winds, from the farthest part of earth to the farthest part of heaven. (Mark 13:24–27)

And there will be signs in the sun, in the moon, and in the stars; and on the earth distress of nations, with perplexity, the sea and the waves roaring; men's hearts failing them from fear and the expectation of those things which are coming on the earth, for the powers of the heavens will be shaken. Then they will see the Son of Man coming in a cloud with power and great glory. Now when these things begin to happen, look up and lift up your heads, because your redemption draws near. (Luke 21:25–28)

I will show wonders in heaven above
And signs in the earth beneath:
Blood and fire and vapor of smoke.
The sun shall be turned into darkness,
And the moon into blood,
Before the coming of the great and awesome day of the LORD.
And it shall come to pass
That whoever calls on the name of the LORD shall be saved.
(Acts 2:19–21)

> And I will show wonders in the heavens and in the earth:
> Blood and fire and pillars of smoke.
> The sun shall be turned into darkness,
> And the moon into blood,
> Before the coming of the great and awesome day of the LORD.
> And it shall come to pass
> That whoever calls on the name of the LORD
> Shall be saved.
> For in Mount Zion and in Jerusalem there shall be deliverance,
> As the LORD has said, among the remnant whom the LORD calls.
> (Joel 2:30–32)

> Multitudes, multitudes in the valley of decision!
> For the day of the LORD is near in the valley of decision.
> The sun and moon will grow dark,
> And the stars will diminish their brightness.
> The LORD also will roar from Zion,
> And utter His voice from Jerusalem;
> The heavens and earth will shake;
> But the LORD will be a shelter for His people,
> And the strength of the children of Israel.
> (Joel 3:14–16)

Behold, I tell you a mystery: we shall not all sleep, but we shall all be changed—in a moment, in the twinkling of an eye, at the last trumpet. For the trumpet will sound, and the dead will be raised incorruptible, and we shall be changed. For this corruptible must put on incorruption, and this mortal must put on immortality. (1 Corinthians 15:51–53)

For the Lord Himself will descend from heaven with a shout, with the voice of an archangel, and with the trumpet of God. And

> the dead in Christ will rise first. Then we who are alive and remain shall be caught up together with them in the clouds to meet the Lord in the air. And thus we shall always be with the Lord. (1 Thessalonians 4:16–17)

There is a sequence of events that will occur before the Rapture according to these Scriptures. The first three-and-a-half years of the Tribulation Israel has signed a peace treaty with the Antichrist and temple worship has been resumed in the third temple in Jerusalem. During this time, the church will be persecuted and martyred at the hands of the Antichrist. During the fifth seal, those who already had been martyred were told to wait until their number was complete. The number of martyrs will be completed at the end of the first three-and-a-half years of Tribulation and then during the sixth seal the Rapture of the church will occur. The seventh seal will begin the punishment and judgment from God upon the ungodly that are left behind. The church is not appointed for the wrath of God, so God's judgment upon the unrighteous does not come until the seventh seal: "For God did not appoint us to wrath, but to obtain salvation through our Lord Jesus Christ, who died for us, that whether we wake or sleep, we should live together with Him" (1 Thessalonians 5:9–10). One must remember that the first three-and-a-half years of the Tribulation upon the saints is not judgment from God's wrath, but wrath from Satan through the Antichrist. The church is not appointed for the wrath of God, but nowhere in Scripture does it say that we will escape the wrath of Satan. If the early church suffered martyrdom and torture at the hands of Nero, Titus, Domitian, and Diocletian, who were all types of the Antichrist, shall the latter church escape the martyrdom and violence of the Antichrist? There will be many Christian martyrs during this period, but all praise belongs to God for He will shorten that time and then rapture His church. Next, the abomination of desolation who is the Antichrist will break the peace treaty with Israel, end the daily sacrifice in the temple in Jerusalem, and will set up an image of him to be worshipped as God.

> Then he shall confirm a covenant with many for one week;
> But in the middle of the week
> He shall bring an end to sacrifice and offering.
> And on the wing of abominations shall be one who makes desolate,
> Even until the consummation, which is determined,
> Is poured out on the desolate. (Daniel 9:27)

Right after the first three-and-a-half-years of the Tribulation, there will be signs in the heavens and the earth to prepare the saints for their departure from this earth. The sun will be darkened, the moon will have a blood red appearance, the brilliance of the stars will fade, and the seas will roar with extraordinary turbulence. Fear will fill the inhabitants of the earth, but the Christians will know that their redemption is near and that Jesus is coming to take them to be with Him. These signs will be given as a warning before Christ comes to those who are in the valley of decision. This will be their final opportunity to accept Jesus Christ as Lord and Savior, or they will have to endure the final seven plagues upon mankind. God's mercy, grace and patience is displayed in these signs, for it is His desire that all should be saved. Next, the loud voice of an archangel that sounds like a trumpet blast will announce the great coming of Jesus and He will appear in the sky. Simultaneously with that trumpet blast, the dead who have accepted Jesus Christ will rise to meet the Lord in the sky. Then those who are alive will rise to meet the Lord in the air and they will be given new incorruptible eternal bodies. These are the Lord's words to me through His Spirit regarding the sixth seal. "*The sixth seal is the time that I will remove My church from the earth. The dead will rise first and then those who are alive will come up. This is also a day of judgment, but it is not the time that I judge the Antichrist, the false prophet or Satan. This is the time that I pronounce judgment on the nations. In every nation, tribe, and tongue they will know that I am Lord. Those that have refused Me will be left here to face the horrific plagues that will come. I have repeatedly warned in Scripture that when the abomination of desolation is set up in the temple, then My return is coming quickly. Child, I want to show you in the Spirit the catching away of My Church. I will show you through one small girl."*

This is the vision that the Holy Spirit gave me. I saw a small girl with long blond hair with a headband holding her hair in place. She had a fair complexion with rounded cheeks and I knew through the Holy Spirit that she was ten years old. I saw her hiding in a dark secluded room, like an attic, and she was reading her Bible by the sunlight that was shining through a small window. She was praying and asking God for strength because her days had been long and lonely. When evening came she retreated to the corner of the attic and curled up to go to sleep. While she was sleeping in this dark room, I saw the entire room being lit up by a brilliant light. The little girl woke and suddenly sat up, shielding her eyes from this brilliant light. Then she heard a tender voice speaking to her: "Come, Amelia, it is time." He reached out his hand and took her small hand in his. All the fear that she had bottled up inside was released the moment her hand touched his and she now felt safe, loved, and protected. Then I saw this brilliantly white garmented person and this small blond-haired girl begin to rise. They went right through the roof of the house as if it were not there. They continued to rise until all I saw was a pinpoint of light radiating from the brilliantly clad man. Next, I had a view of Amelia up close as they continued to rise. She was looking with amazement at her arms and she kept touching them and patting them over and over. Then she noticed that her legs also had a different appearance. Amelia also was stunned by her hair that seemed to be glowing. She was no longer wearing the clothes she went to bed in, but now she had on a shimmering white dress that was fastened at the waist with a gold belt. They continued to rise together into the heavens. Then I saw a dark sky full of sparkling lights rising up, and by His Spirit I knew that each light was a child of God being escorted to heaven by an angel in the catching away of the church. The vision of this dark sky filled with these radiant bright lights was so magnificent! The view was more breathtaking and awe inspiring than the Northern Lights, because they were the precious people of every tribe, nation, and tongue rising to meet the One they called Lord Jesus Christ.

REVELATION 7:1–8

> After these things I saw four angels standing at the four corners of the earth, holding the four winds of the earth, that the wind should not blow on the earth, on the sea, or on any tree. Then I saw another angel ascending from the east, having the seal of the living God. And he cried with a loud voice to the four angels to whom it was granted to harm the earth and the sea, saying, "Do not harm the earth, the sea, or the trees till we have sealed the servants of our God on their foreheads." And I heard the number of those who were sealed. One hundred and forty-four thousand of all the tribes of the children of Israel were sealed:
>
> of the tribe of Judah twelve thousand were sealed;
> of the tribe of Reuben twelve thousand were sealed;
> of the tribe of Gad twelve thousand were sealed;
> of the tribe of Asher twelve thousand were sealed;
> of the tribe of Naphtali twelve thousand were sealed;
> of the tribe of Manasseh twelve thousand were sealed;
> of the tribe of Simeon twelve thousand were sealed;
> of the tribe of Levi twelve thousand were sealed;
> of the tribe of Issachar twelve thousand were sealed;
> of the tribe of Zebulun twelve thousand were sealed;
> of the tribe of Joseph twelve thousand were sealed;
> of the tribe of Benjamin twelve thousand were sealed.

Right after the rapture of the church, John heard that there were one hundred and forty-four thousand Jews that were given the seal of God. There were twelve thousand men each from the twelve tribes of Israel and these were the Lord's firstfruits that were redeemed from Israel. The biblical concept of firstfruits can be understood by studying the Old Testament feast day called the Sheaf of Firstfruits. When Israel entered into the Promised Land, they were commanded by God to keep the feast day Sheaf of Firstfruits. During their time of wandering in the wilderness, God fed the Israelites manna, but upon entering the Promised Land, they would harvest their own crops. During the harvest period under Passover and Pentecost, a person would take one of the sheaves of the standing harvest of barley and wheat before the crops were reaped. He would present this lone sheaf to the priest who would wave it before the Lord as an offering. This sheaf was a representative or symbol of the coming harvest and was always the choicest, the best, and the most excellent of all that was to follow. The firstfruits were always holy to the Lord. Jesus Christ's fulfillment as the Firstfruit was accomplished when He became the unsurpassed perfect holy Lamb of God, and His resurrection would signify the coming harvest of souls. The Sheaf of Firstfruits is an amazing prophetic type of the resurrection of Christ. Just as Christ was the firstfruit of all who would have resurrection life through Him, the one hundred and forty-four thousand Israelites are the Lord's firstfruits that have been set aside by Him before the whole nation of Israel is saved. These are the Lord's words to me regarding this: *"Before My final judgment of the earth, I will gather one hundred and forty-four thousand from the twelve tribes of Israel. They are My firstfruits that I have redeemed from Israel. After this takes place, all of Israel will be saved."* "And so all Israel will be saved, as it is written: "The 'Deliverer will come out of Zion, / and He will turn away ungodliness from Jacob; / for this is My covenant with them, when I take away their sins'" (Romans 11:26–27). "But Israel shall be saved by the LORD with an everlasting salvation; you shall not be ashamed or disgraced forever and ever" (Isaiah 45:17).

The twelve tribes of Israel that are listed in Revelation chapter seven do not include all the original twelve tribes of Israel listed in Genesis chapter forty-nine. At the closing of Genesis, Jacob was dying and he gathered his twelve sons around him and prophesied over each one. To Joseph he said: "Moreover I have given to you one portion above your brothers, which I took from the hand of the Amorite with my sword and my bow"

(Genesis 48:22). Joseph was given a double portion of inheritance over his brothers by his father Israel. This prophecy is evidenced in Revelation because Joseph's oldest son Manasseh is listed as one the twelve tribes along with Joseph. In Revelation, the tribe of Dan is omitted because Jacob prophesied this over his son Dan: "Dan shall be a serpent by the way, a viper by the path, that bites the horse's heels so that its rider shall fall backward" (Genesis 49:17). Compare this prophecy regarding Dan with the prophecy that the Lord God spoke to the serpent in the Garden of Eden. I have placed the words in brackets for emphasis. "And I will put enmity between you [Satan] and the woman, [Israel] and between your seed [Antichrist] and her Seed; [Jesus Christ] He [Jesus Christ] shall bruise your head, and you [Satan] shall bruise His [Christ's] heel" (Genesis 3:15). In this Scripture God pronounced that there would be enmity between Satan and Israel and there would be enmity between the seed of Satan who is the Antichrist and Israel's Seed who is Jesus Christ. Satan bruised Christ's heel by using His people to condemn Him to death, and Christ bruised the head of Satan by conquering sin through His death and resurrection. A blow to the head is much more fatal than a blow to the foot, and this is the blow that Satan received through Jesus Christ's death and resurrection. Returning to the prophetic words that were spoken over Dan, he is called a serpent which is a reference to Satan. Dan is said to be a serpent that bites the horse's heels and this is very similar to Satan bruising the heel of Christ. The reason that Dan is called a serpent and is not listed as a tribe in Revelation is because the Antichrist will arise from the tribe of Dan. In order for the Antichrist to be accepted by Israel as the real Christ, he must be a Jew. There was another prophesy made by Moses that substantiates the Antichrist will descend from the tribe of Dan. It was prophesied by Moses that the tribe of Dan would give birth to a lion: "And of Dan he said: 'Dan is a lion's whelp' (Deuteronomy 33:22). The lion that Dan would produce would be the Antichrist, a counterfeit of Christ. It says in Scripture that the devil walks about like a roaring lion; he is not the actual lion because he is a counterfeit. "Be sober, be vigilant; because your adversary the devil walks about like a roaring lion, seeking whom he may devour" (1Peter 5:8). Jesus Christ is the true Lion from the Tribe of Judah. "Judah is a lion's whelp;...the scepter shall not depart from Judah" (Genesis 49:9–10). "...Behold, the Lion of the tribe of Judah, the Root of David, has prevailed to open the scroll and to loose its seven seals" (Revelation 5:5). From Scripture it is evident that the tribe of Judah would bring forth a Lion of the tribe of Judah, Jesus Christ; and the tribe of Dan would bring forth a roaring lion, the Antichrist. Jeremiah also prophesied that the Antichrist would come from the tribe of Dan.

> For a voice declares from Dan
> And proclaims affliction from Mount Ephraim:
> "Make mention to the nations,
> Yes, proclaim against Jerusalem,
> That watchers come from a far country
> And raise their voice against the cities of Judah.
> Like keepers of a field they are against her all around,
> Because she has been rebellious against Me," says the LORD.
> (Jeremiah 4:15–17)

Jeremiah prophesied that there would be a voice from the tribe of Dan that would make proclamations against Jerusalem. He would announce this from Mount Ephraim, which is a central mountain range extending from Bethel to the Plain of Jezreel. The proclamation that he will make is that watchers will come from a far country and gather in a field to come against the cities of Judah. The Hebrew word for "watcher" in this context is *nat sar*, which means "to be concealed and hidden, to besiege, and to guard in a bad sense." This announcement that will come from the voice of the Antichrist will be fulfilled when the armies from a far country will gather in the Jezreel Plain during the final Battle of Armageddon. Scriptures not only give us the genealogical heritage of the Antichrist, they also reveal what territory he will come from. The book of Daniel identifies the

Antichrist as the king of the North and that he will not regard the God of his fathers which also indicates that he is a Jew.

> He shall regard neither the God of his fathers nor the desire of women, nor regard any god; for he shall exalt himself above them all. But in their place he shall honor a god of fortresses; and a god which his fathers did not know he shall honor with gold and silver, with precious stones and pleasant things. Thus he shall act against the strongest fortresses with a foreign god, which he shall acknowledge, and advance its glory; and he shall cause them to rule over many, and divide the land for gain. At the time of the end the king of the South shall attack him; and the king of the North shall come against him like a whirlwind, with chariots, horsemen, and with many ships; and he shall enter the countries, overwhelm them, and pass through. He shall also enter the Glorious Land, and many countries shall be overthrown. (Daniel 11:37–41)

These are the Lord's words to me: *"These Scriptures have been opened up to you by My Spirit. The Antichrist will be a Jew from the tribe of Dan. My Word in Daniel states that the Antichrist is from the north which is the land of Syria."*

Revelation 7:9–17

> After these things I looked, and behold, a great multitude which no one could number, of all nations, tribes, peoples, and tongues, standing before the throne and before the Lamb, clothed with white robes, with palm branches in their hands, and crying out with a loud voice, saying, "Salvation belongs to our God who sits on the throne, and to the Lamb!" All the angels stood around the throne and the elders and the four living creatures, and fell on their faces before the throne and worshiped God, saying:

> "Amen! Blessing and glory and wisdom,
> thanksgiving and honor and power and might,
> be to our God forever and ever,
> Amen."
>
> Then one of the elders answered, saying to me, "Who are these arrayed in white robes, and where did they come from?" And I said to him, "Sir, you know." So he said to me, "These are the ones who come out of the great tribulation, and washed their robes and made them white in the blood of the Lamb. Therefore they are before the throne of God, and serve Him day and night in His temple. And He who sits on the throne will dwell among them. They shall neither hunger anymore nor thirst anymore; the sun shall not strike them, nor any heat; for the Lamb who is in the midst of the throne will shepherd them and lead them to living fountains of waters. And God will wipe away every tear from their eyes.

This beautiful scene of people from every nation, tribe, and tongue worshipping around the throne of God is the multitude that came out of the Great Tribulation. Those that were martyred during the Tribulation as well as those who were taken up to heaven in the Rapture were seen worshipping around the throne of God and to each one was given a white robe. Every need is met by the Lord Jesus Christ as He shepherds His people and wipes every tear from the eyes of His beloved children. The Lord will not return for His church until the gospel has been preached to every tribe, tongue and nation. This panoramic view of the nations worshipping around the throne of God happens after the church has proclaimed the gospel message to every tribe, tongue and nation. "And the gospel must first be preached to all the nations" (Mark 13:10). The Holy Spirit said this to me: "*I will show you a vision of all the tribes, nations, and tongues worshipping around the throne.*" In the Spirit, I saw a great and very tall angel place a golden trumpet to his lips. He gave the trumpet three great blasts that could be heard from a great distance. I saw people frolicking on green grassy knolls when they heard the trumpet blasts, and the multitude of people moved toward the sound of the trumpet to gather around the throne of God. All I saw of the throne was a radiant bright light reflecting off what looked like a glass floor. Beams of light were radiating and shooting out like a laser light show. Then I was in a position where I was viewing this multitude of people face to face, and I noticed the pure joy and bliss on their faces. I was shown some individual faces and I will describe what I saw. I saw a Chinese man with high rounded cheeks with a smile that lit up his face and eyes. I saw an American Indian with long black hair, a deep bronze complexion, his dark eyes were dancing with sparkling lights, and his look and countenance was so tender. I saw a tall blond woman with cornflower blue eyes and she was twirling like a ballerina. I saw a very dark-skinned black man and I knew by the Holy Spirit that he was from an African tribe. His toothy grin stood out against his dark skin and his eyes were so full of love and tenderness. I saw a man of short stature that had dark brown skin and black hair and I knew that he was from India. His eyes were laughing as he was lifting up his hands in praise. Then I saw a beautiful Philippino woman with perfect brown skin and a smile that reached her eyes and reflected her inner beauty. What stood out in this vision were the eyes of these people and the Spirit of God said this: "*The eye is the window to the spirit. Make the eye good and the whole body is good.*" There was an entire sea of faces of every nationality before me, and the common thread was that they all had a blissful look upon their faces and they were all wearing white robes tied at the waist. Then all of the sudden, this multitude of people from every tribe, nation, and tongue began to worship simultaneously. No one cued them or was directing them. They were worshipping in perfect harmony and the range of their voices was a phenomenal blend. The magnitude and variety of voices was magnificent as they sang in one continuous song without pauses and without a beat to the music. They were all singing in one language—one that I did not recognize. Next, I saw something that was truly amazing. Without a prompt, they all raised their hands in praise in total unison. They were truly one body worshipping God in Spirit and in Truth. The last face that I was shown in this vision brought tears to my eyes because of what was spoken to me. I saw a man with long locks and I knew that he was an Israeli Jew. His face was especially tender, and his brown eyes were beckoning to me as he spoke these words: "Go to my brethren and tell them about Yeshua."

Chapter Four

Seven Final Plagues

Revelation chapter eight begins the judgments of God that are poured out upon the inhabitants of earth who have been left behind. These judgments are contained within the seventh seal and are called the seven trumpets, which are the seven last plagues. In Revelation chapters fifteen and sixteen there are also seven judgments called the seven bowls. When looking at both the seven trumpets and the seven bowls, one can determine there are similarities between them, and yet some distinct differences. The Lord Jesus revealed this to me regarding the seven trumpets and the seven bowls. "*The seventh seal is the seal of completion. Within this seal are seven trumpets that are sounded by seven angels. The seven trumpets are indeed the same as the seven bowls; for they are My final seven plagues upon men which make My wrath complete. John saw these seven plagues twice and he recorded them as he viewed them. Child, I repeat events in Scripture so they are not missed. That is the reason there are so many prophecies recorded in the First Testament about Me; so My first coming would not be missed. John was shown the last seven plagues twice because two is the number of witness.*" There was also another time in Scripture that God revealed a particular event twice to cause the people to know that the thing would surely happen. Joseph was a slave in Egypt and Pharaoh had two dreams of the same event. He dreamed there were seven fat cows and seven lean cows and the gaunt cows ate up the fat cows. He dreamed a second time and seven plump heads of grain were devoured by seven thin blighted heads of wheat. This dream was interpreted by Joseph that God had revealed Egypt would have seven years of plenty followed by seven years of famine. Joseph says this about the dream: "And the dream was repeated to Pharaoh twice because the thing is established by God, and God will shortly bring it to pass" (Genesis 41:32). The seven last plagues in Revelation are repeated twice because they are established by God and God will bring them to pass. In light of what the Lord revealed regarding the trumpets and the bowls, they will be studied simultaneously in order to get the greatest insight. Therefore, Revelation chapters eight and nine will be deliberated side by side with Revelation chapters fifteen and sixteen.

REVELATION 8:1–2

> "When He opened the seventh seal, there was silence in heaven for about half an hour. And I saw the seven angels who stand before God, and to them were given seven trumpets."

REVELATION 15:1

> "Then I saw another sign in heaven, great and marvelous: seven angels having the seven last plagues, for in them the wrath of God is complete."

Jesus opened the seventh seal and there was complete silence in heaven. This holy reverential fear had overcome heaven's inhabitants because they knew that God's wrath was about to be poured out upon the inhabitants of the earth. Seven angels were given seven trumpets to sound and when the blast of the horn was sounded, seven different angels poured the wrath of God out from their bowls. Keeping in mind that the seven trumpets are the seven angels announcing the plague and the seven bowls are the actual pouring out of the plague, then it is easy to reconcile that the trumpets and the bowls are the same. These plagues that were about to be poured out reveal that God does take vengeance on people and nations that continually refuse to recognize Him as God. All throughout Scripture,

God has used wars, captivity, death, droughts, diseases, and plagues to discipline those who refuse to obey Him. There are those who would say that their God is a God of love and He would never do such things. They also tout that God only did those things in the Old Testament. God does not change; He still disciplines rebellious people. The only difference is that people refuse to believe that it is God's hand of judgment; for if they acknowledged that it was His judgment, they would be found guilty. God still uses wars, hurricanes, plagues, tsunamis, earthquakes and droughts to display His wrath to sinful man.

> Thus says the LORD to this people:
> "Thus they have loved to wander;
> They have not restrained their feet.
> Therefore the LORD does not accept them;
> He will remember their iniquity now,
> And punish their sins."
>
> Then the LORD said to me, "Do not pray for this people, for their good. When they fast, I will not hear their cry; and when they offer burnt offering and grain offering, I will not accept them. But I will consume them by the sword, by the famine, and by the pestilence." (Jeremiah 14:10–12)

REVELATION 8:3–6

> Then another angel, having a golden censer, came and stood at the altar. He was given much incense, that he should offer it with the prayers of all the saints upon the golden altar which was before the throne. And the smoke of the incense, with the prayers of the saints, ascended before God from the angel's hand. Then the angel took the censer, filled it with fire from the altar, and threw it to the earth. And there were noises, thunderings, lightnings, and an earthquake. So the seven angels who had the seven trumpets prepared themselves to sound.

REVELATION 15:2–8

> And I saw something like a sea of glass mingled with fire, and those who have the victory over the beast, over his image and over his mark and over the number of his name, standing on the sea of glass, having harps of God. They sing the song of Moses, the servant of God, and the song of the Lamb, saying:
>
> "Great and marvelous are Your works,
> Lord God Almighty!
> Just and true are Your ways,
> O King of the saints!
> Who shall not fear You, O Lord, and glorify Your name?
> For You alone are holy.
> For all nations shall come and worship before You,
> For Your judgments have been manifested."
>
> After these things I looked, and behold, the temple of the tabernacle of the testimony in heaven was opened. And out of the temple came the seven angels having the seven plagues, clothed in pure bright linen, and having their chests girded with golden bands. Then one of the four living creatures gave to the seven angels seven golden bowls full of the wrath of God who lives forever and ever. The temple was filled with smoke from the glory of God and from His power, and no one was able to enter the temple till the seven plagues of the seven angels were completed.

A multitude who overcame the Antichrist and the false prophet by losing their lives was seen singing around the magnificent throne of God. The song of the saints is very notable because they proclaimed God's marvelous works, His holiness, and His manifest judgments upon the earth. Worshipping the Lord in Spirit and truth by proclaiming His greatness through music is one of the highest forms of worship there is. Worship ushers us into the presence of God when our focus is entirely on Him. God created man to be a tri-part being of spirit, soul, and body. The spirit is the only part of man that can connect with God. The soul is comprised of the mind, the will, and the emotions; and the body is the physical part that we can see and touch. When sin entered into the world, man began operating from his soulish realm because the spirit connection with God had been severed. Jesus Christ's death on the cross removed our sins and restored our severed relationship with God so that we could worship Him in our spirits, which is the only part of man that can be joined with God. True worship is when our spirits are elevated to their correct place of dominion over the soul and body and we become one with God. Jesus answered the Samaritan woman's question about the place where one ought to worship and at the same time identified Himself as the Messiah.

> You worship what you do not know; we know what we worship, for salvation is of the Jews. But the hour is coming, and now is, when the true worshipers will worship the Father in spirit and truth; for the Father is seeking such to worship Him. God is Spirit, and those who worship Him must worship in spirit and truth." The woman said to Him, "I know that Messiah is coming" (who is called Christ). "When He comes, He will tell us all things." Jesus said to her, "I who speak to you am He." (John 4:22–26)

In essence, Jesus was telling her that unless she acknowledged Him as the Messiah, then she would not be able to worship God, because the place to worship was not a location. The place to worship God was the renewed spirit within man that occurs when a person receives Jesus Christ as Messiah. When a person worships God in Spirit and in truth, the spiritual part of our tri-part beings becomes one with God and the communion is so beautiful. If you truly are seeking to be one with God and desire Him to reveal Himself to you, then set time aside to worship Him. Worship the Lord with praise music, by singing, dancing, bowing down, lying prostrate on the floor, singing in tongues, reading psalms, and proclaiming how great He is. We express our love through worship and it touches the heart of God. King David was a lover of God and expressed his love with psalms, songs, musical instruments, and dancing. David joyously worshipped God when the ark was being brought back to Jerusalem and he danced in the streets whirling around, kicking up his feet while playing a musical instrument. God looks with delight at worship that is done with such complete abandonment of self. When I am alone with God, I love to worship Him with this kind of zeal because I can I abandon myself to the pure joy of adoration to my Lord. I even have worshipped the Lord in the middle of a golf course when the course is closed for the evening. There are a series of mounded hills on the fairway that I cross over during my walk and I have danced on these hills to the Lord while my praise music is resonating in my ears. I express my love to the Lord by dancing, twirling, and leaping while the songs of worship reach the depths of my spirit, and my voice bellows out the words of praise. Through unadulterated worship, my spirit is joined intimately with the life-giving Spirit of the Lord and it allows His vitality, His nature, and His power to flow through me. This union with Him makes me complete and no one else can take His place to fulfill that oneness. I was created to worship the Lord. You were created to worship the Lord. When you worship Jesus from the depths of your spirit, He can transform you so that you become one with Him. Through worship, the believer is joined to the Lord which clothes us with the victory of Christ and gives us the knowledge of His will and mind. There is great victory in praising and glorifying the Lord through song, because battles are won in the spiritual realm so that we don't have to fight. God fights for us.

> And he said, "Listen, all you of Judah and you inhabitants of Jerusalem, and you, King Jehoshaphat! Thus says the LORD to

> you: 'Do not be afraid nor dismayed because of this great multitude, for the battle is not yours, but God's.... You will not need to fight in this battle. Position yourselves, stand still and see the salvation of the LORD, who is with you, O Judah and Jerusalem!' Do not fear or be dismayed; tomorrow go out against them, for the LORD is with you." ...And when he had consulted with the people, he appointed those who should sing to the LORD, and who should praise the beauty of holiness, as they went out before the army and were saying: "Praise the LORD, for His mercy endures forever." Now when they began to sing and to praise, the LORD set ambushes against the people of Ammon, Moab, and Mount Seir, who had come against Judah; and they were defeated. (2 Chronicles 20:15, 17, 21–22)

Jehoshaphat understood the importance of worshipping God when he was coming up against a formidable enemy. Against all odds, the battle was won through the power of God and Judah never had to lift a hand in the battle, just their voices in praise. Satan is a formidable enemy and when he comes against us through circumstances and situations in our lives, our response should be that we worship God. How many times do we whine and complain to God about our circumstances and then call this whining a prayer? True triumph over the situation comes through worshipping God. I have done my fair share of whining and pleading with God only to realize that my true victory came through worshipping Him. There is so much victory in praising God during these battles because He is our Defender, Protector, and Deliverer. Paul and Silas knew the power of praising God in dire circumstances. They had just been beaten with thirty-nine stripes, and with their flesh ripped open and their feet in stocks, they sat on the prison floor and raised their voices in songs of praise. "But at midnight Paul and Silas were praying and singing hymns to God, and the prisoners were listening to them. Suddenly there was a great earthquake, so that the foundations of the prison were shaken; and immediately all the doors were opened and everyone's chains were loosed" (Acts 16:25–26). As a result of Silas and Paul's singing and prayer, the prison door flew wide open and everyone's chains were loosed. Silas and Paul's worship set the prisoners free from their bondage. Through the power of worshipping God, people are set free from the bondage of sin, sickness and sorrow, and the grip of Satan is destroyed. Praise God! There truly is victory in worshipping God! In heaven, John was shown that this victory continues throughout all eternity while the saints continue their worship around the throne of God.

The heavenly tabernacle was opened and the seven angels having the seven plagues came out of the temple. One of the seraphim who were around the throne of God day and night proclaiming the holiness of God gave these angels the bowls of the wrath of God. The Lord Jesus spoke these words to me: *"It is one of My Holy ones that gives the seven angels My bowls of wrath to be poured out. My heavenly tabernacle is uninhabitable during these final bowls of wrath because My Father's power and glory fill the temple. Neither the saints nor the angels can enter the temple because His power and glory are magnified beyond all ability to stand in His Presence. No one knows His great power but Me."*

FIRST TRUMPET—REVELATION 8:7

"The first angel sounded: And hail and fire followed, mingled with blood, and they were thrown to the earth. And a third of the trees were burned up, and all green grass was burned up."

FIRST BOWL—REVELATION 16:1–2

"Then I heard a loud voice from the temple saying to the seven angels, 'Go and pour out the bowls of the wrath of God on the earth.' So the first went and poured out his bowl upon the earth, and a foul and loathsome sore came upon the men who had the mark of the beast and those who worshiped his image."

This first plague had hail and fire mingled with blood. The result of this plague was one third of the trees and grass was burned up and men that have taken the mark of the Beast break out in loathsome sores. Those who get saved after the Rapture and have not taken the mark of the Beast will not suffer with these loathsome sores. Just as God made a distinction between the Israelites and the Egyptians during the ten plagues, He will also make a distinction between His people and those who belong to Satan. The Lord spoke these words to me regarding this first plague. *"Child, it is blood of the martyrs mingled with the hail and fire that causes the loathsome sores to be upon men. I have granted revenge to those martyrs that cried out from under My altar. Their blood has been mixed with fire and hail and thrown to the earth to avenge their deaths."*

Second Trumpet—Revelation 8:8–9

> "Then the second angel sounded: And something like a great mountain burning with fire was thrown into the sea, and a third of the sea became blood. And a third of the living creatures in the sea died, and a third of the ships were destroyed."

Second Bowl—Revelation 16:3

> "Then the second angel poured out his bowl on the sea, and it became blood as of a dead man; and every living creature in the sea died."

This is the Lord's explanation of the second trumpet and the second bowl. *"John was witnessing a volcano erupting in the Aegean Sea. I have reserved this volcano for such a day as this and the sounding of My angel releases it to erupt. This earth from the ages past to the ages future will never see such destruction from a volcano. One third of the sea life and ships will be destroyed in the Aegean Sea. Remember that John was witnessing the same event twice. It was the same sea that he saw the second time. Initially only one third of the sea creatures died because of the volcanic eruption, but because of the contamination of blood, all the rest died. Therefore the second time I showed John this plague, all the sea creatures have died. Scriptures never contradict. Just as the gospel writers wrote from a different view of the same event, John has seen this volcano erupt and viewed it at different intervals.* I asked the Lord why He chose the Aegean Sea and not another one and His response was this: "*Child, all of My judgments in the form of these plagues are very specifically addressing sin. The sin that I am punishing with this plague is unbelief. My servant Paul established many churches around the Aegean Sea. I warned every one of those churches through My servant John and yet not one of those churches obeyed. I have indeed removed their lampstand. Let this be a warning to churches today. Heed My Word!*" It is worthy to note that the seven churches that Jesus addressed in the beginning of Revelation were all located in Asia Minor that borders the Aegean Sea, along with the Colossian and the Galatian churches. The Philippian, the Thessalonian and the Corinthian churches were also on the opposite coast of the Aegean Sea. Another amazing fact is that currently a large volcano is sitting in the Aegean Sea on a southernmost island named Thera. Between 1500 B.C. and 1620 B.C., one of the largest volcanic eruptions known to man erupted on Thera from this volcano. From scientific discoveries found in the layers of the earth, ash and pumice have been found as far away as Egypt and Israel due to this ancient eruption. The Lord has revealed that He has reserved a horrific volcano for this second trumpet and bowl, and this dreadfully large volcano sits in the Aegean Sea. God is the great I AM who reveals!

THIRD TRUMPET—REVELATION 8:10–11

> "Then the third angel sounded: And a great star fell from heaven, burning like a torch, and it fell on a third of the rivers and on the springs of water. The name of the star is Wormwood. A third of the waters became wormwood, and many men died from the water, because it was made bitter."

THIRD BOWL—REVELATION 16:4-5

"Then the third angel poured out his bowl on the rivers and springs of water, and they became blood. And I heard the angel of the waters saying: "You are righteous, O Lord the One who is and who was and who is to be, because You have judged these things."

The Lord's revelation about this third trumpet and bowl is this: "*The great star from heaven is My angel released to make the fresh water bitter. The angel's name is Wormwood which means to make bitter. Men will drink from the water before they know it is poisonous. The poison also will kill the fresh water fish, which turns the water to blood. Again, John saw the same event two separate times. This plague is also one that vindicates the shed blood of My saints and prophets. The martyred saints and prophets heartily agree with My judgments; for My judgments are true and just.*"

FOURTH TRUMPET—REVELATION 8:12–13

"Then the fourth angel sounded: And a third of the sun was struck, a third of the moon, and a third of the stars, so that a third of them were darkened. A third of the day did not shine, and likewise the night. And I looked, and I heard an angel flying through the midst of heaven, saying with a loud voice, "Woe, woe, woe to the inhabitants of the earth, because of the remaining blasts of the trumpet of the three angels who are about to sound!"

FOURTH BOWL—REVELATION 16:8–9

"Then the fourth angel poured out his bowl on the sun, and power was given to him to scorch men with fire. And men were scorched with great heat, and they blasphemed the name of God who has power over these plagues; and they did not repent and give Him glory."

The Lord revealed this about the fourth trumpet and bowl. *"John witnessed cosmic disturbances regarding the sun and the moon and the stars. Because of these cosmic disturbances, people will be looking to the skies when My angel announces, "Woe, Woe, Woe, to the inhabitants of the earth." By now, those left on earth know that it is God who is sending these plagues upon them. But they do not repent and they continue to curse Me. I have given My angel power to scorch men with fire and heat from the sun. I have set the sun, moon, and stars on My path and now they have been taken off their course as My judgment. The sin that is being judged with this plague is the sin of blasphemy."* God is the Creator of the heavens and the earth and He has set the sun, the moon, and the stars on their path and He has the power to change them.

> Of old You laid the foundation of the earth,
> And the heavens are the work of Your hands.
> They will perish, but You will endure;
> Yes, they will all grow old like a garment;
> Like a cloak You will change them, and they will be changed.
> (Psalm 102:25–26)

FIFTH TRUMPET—REVELATION 9:1–12

> Then the fifth angel sounded: And I saw a star fallen from heaven to the earth. To him was given the key to the bottomless pit. And he opened the bottomless pit, and smoke arose out of the pit like the smoke of a great furnace. So the sun and the air were darkened because of the smoke of the pit. Then out of the smoke locusts came upon the earth. And to them was given power, as the scorpions of the earth have power. They were commanded not to harm the grass of the earth, or any green thing, or any tree, but only those men who do not have the seal of God on their foreheads. And they were not given authority to kill them, but to torment them for five months. Their torment was like the torment of a scorpion when it strikes a man. In those days men will seek

death and will not find it; they will desire to die, and death will flee from them. The shape of the locusts was like horses prepared for battle. On their heads were crowns of something like gold, and their faces were like the faces of men. They had hair like women's hair, and their teeth were like lions' teeth. And they had breastplates like breastplates of iron, and the sound of their wings was like the sound of chariots with many horses running into battle. They had tails like scorpions, and there were stings in their tails. Their power was to hurt men five months. And they had as king over them the angel of the bottomless pit, whose name in Hebrew is Abaddon, but in Greek he has the name Apollyon. One woe is past. Behold, still two more woes are coming after these things.

FIFTH BOWL—REVELATION 16:10–11

"Then the fifth angel poured out his bowl on the throne of the beast, and his kingdom became full of darkness; and they gnawed their tongues because of the pain. They blasphemed the God of heaven because of their pains and their sores, and did not repent of their deeds."

The Lord revealed this about the fifth trumpet and bowl: *"It is My angel that unlocks the bottomless pit to release these demonic beings. These demons were locked in the bottomless pit and reserved for this time by My authority. These demons have been given authority to torment men for five months who do not have the seal of God; but they do not have the authority to kill them."* The Lord further described to me the torment and pain that these demons inflicted upon men. *"Their bodies will feel like they are on fire. In every joint there will be excruciating pain. There will be no relief from the pain and medicines will not relieve it. Do you remember the excruciating sciatic pain you experienced? Multiply that pain, but all over the entire body."* John compared the outward appearance of these demons to familiar objects that he knew.

Their shape was like a horse prepared for battle, they had crowns upon their heads, and they had human looking faces. They had long hair like a woman's, sharp teeth like lions', and a breastplate that covered their chests. They had wings with which they flew and tails like a scorpion to sting men. These demons were real and John employed the comparison method to describe a totally unfamiliar object with things he was familiar with. The Lord also explained to me about the physical appearance of these demons. *"The size of these demons is the size of a locust, the size of a cicada. The outward physical characteristics of these demons depict the ways that man has sinned. The horses prepared for battle represent man's independence, rather than depending on Me. For this reason, I did not permit My chosen people to have horses for battle. When I took them into battle, they had to rely on Me for victory and not rely on their own strength. The crown of gold on the demon's head represents bowing down to earthly kings instead of bowing down to the Lord of lords and King of kings. The face of a man represents attaining knowledge without having knowledge of the Holy One of God. The woman's hair represents sexual sin in all its depravity: fornication, adultery, homosexuality, rape, incest, and bestiality. The lion's teeth represent man's cruelty toward one another: war, murder, unjust imprisonment, torture, abortion, and euthanasia. The breastplate of iron represents the world system. Men chose to follow the ways of Egypt instead of My way. The wings which sounded like chariots with many horses represent man's flight from God. Instead of mounting up with wings like eagles, they will ascend into the bottomless pit from whence these demons have come. The tails of scorpions represent the sting of death, over which the second death will have power. The final demise of those tortured by these demons will be the bottomless pit and Satan their king will join them."*

SIXTH TRUMPET—REVELATION 9:13–21

> Then the sixth angel sounded: And I heard a voice from the four horns of the golden altar which is before God, saying to the sixth angel who had the trumpet, "Release the four angels who are bound at the great river Euphrates." So the four angels, who had been pre-

pared for the hour and day and month and year, were released to kill a third of mankind. Now the number of the army of the horsemen was two hundred million; I heard the number of them. And thus I saw the horses in the vision: those who sat on them had breastplates of fiery red, hyacinth blue, and sulfur yellow; and the heads of the horses were like the heads of lions; and out of their mouths came fire, smoke, and brimstone. By these three plagues a third of mankind was killed—by the fire and the smoke and the brimstone which came out of their mouths. For their power is in their mouth and in their tails; for their tails are like serpents, having heads; and with them they do harm. But the rest of mankind, who were not killed by these plagues, did not repent of the works of their hands, that they should not worship demons, and idols of gold, silver, brass, stone, and wood, which can neither see nor hear nor walk. And they did not repent of their murders or their sorceries or their sexual immorality or their thefts.

SIXTH BOWL—REVELATION 16:12–16

Then the sixth angel poured out his bowl on the great river Euphrates, and its water was dried up, so that the way of the kings from the east might be prepared. And I saw three unclean spirits like frogs coming out of the mouth of the dragon, out of the mouth of the beast, and out of the mouth of the false prophet. For they are spirits of demons, performing signs, which go out to the kings of the earth and of the whole world, to gather them to the battle of that great day of God Almighty. "Behold, I am coming as a thief. Blessed is he who watches, and keeps his garments, lest he walk naked and they see his shame." And they gathered them together to the place called in Hebrew, Armageddon."

The Lord Jesus revealed this about the sixth trumpet and sixth bowl: "*The voice from the four horns is the voice of the four living creatures that Ezekiel saw. They are My holy anointed ones that are ever present before My throne. My holy ones announce to the sixth angel to release the four angels that have held the Euphrates within its banks. The great river Euphrates water will be released and the river will dry up so that men may walk on the dry river bed. I placed these four angels at the great river Euphrates and prepared them for this exact time in history. The three unclean spirits that proceed out of Satan, the Antichrist and the False Prophet have also been reserved for this exact time in history. These three unclean spirits have the power to persuade the ten nations and the entire world to rebel against Me. They will gather in the plain of Megiddo for that final and awful Battle of Armageddon. Because of deceiving signs and wonders, this trio will be able to convince the nations that they can overcome Me. The army that John viewed is the army that will gather to do battle against Me and that number is 200 million. There will be nations that refuse to join with the Antichrist and he has been given power to kill one third of the remaining mankind with fire, smoke, and brimstone. Rockets, missiles and warheads will be launched at these nations. Child, you saw this in the vision that I showed you in Israel. I showed you the armies gathered together in the Jezreel Plain. The sins that are being judged by this plague of fire, smoke, and brimstone are idolatry, murder, sexual immorality and theft."* When I was in Israel the Lord showed me in a vision the ten nations that will gather their armies in the Jezreel Plain for this final Battle of Armageddon. While viewing the Jezreel Plain from on top of Mount Carmel, the Lord instructed me to visually divide the plain into four quadrants. Within each of the four quadrants, He showed me various uniformed men and identified each of the ten nations according to the color, style, and emblems on their army attire. When viewing these armies from an elevated position, there were so many men that they looked like a swarm of locusts covering the land. There were missiles set up in the plain and I could see them being launched. I also saw small black stealth-like aircraft that resembled a boomerang and these unmanned aircraft were operated from the ground. The Lord revealed to me that these aircraft had been supplied to Israel by the United States but were now in the hands of the enemy because the airfield located in the Jezreel Plain had been breached by Israel's enemies. According to NASA, Boeing is working on a combat air system called the X-45 which is an Unmanned Combat Ariel Vehicle being developed for strike missions. Although Unmanned Ariel Combat Vehicles have been developed with the capability to drop unguided weapons, the future UACV's that I saw in this vision had the capability to release guided missiles. In this vision, I was also given a quick glimpse of the face of the Antichrist and the face of the False Prophet during this final battle. From what I saw in this vision, I can say without a doubt that the Antichrist is of Middle Eastern descent. He had a well-trimmed beard and mustache and a very appealing outward physical appearance. The False Prophet that I saw in the vision had black skin and was of African descent.

The Lord also showed me the spiritual battle that is being waged over the Plain of Megiddo. "*I want to show you more on the Battle of Armageddon. Fear not, I am with you. I want to show you the aerial battle that is being fought as a spiritual battle. This piece of land has been a constant battleground in the spiritual realm. Many physical battles have been fought here as a result of the battle that rages in the spiritual realm. Satan, My chief enemy, knows the importance of this piece of land. He has told his minions that they must maintain control of this battlefield so he can rule and reign in Israel. Satan has convinced his demonic forces that the Book of Revelation is a lie. The battle rages for this land even as you pray. Now I want to show you in the Spirit the battle for the Jezreel Plain. Do not fear, child. I will lift you up so you can walk among the battle.*" This is what I saw and heard when the Lord took me in the Spirit to this battlefield. I saw large, thick, heavy swords clashing against one another so that sparks flew from the metal. The noise was tremendously loud with the fighting and clanking, and I also heard ugly guttural noises coming from the demons. Then one of the demons noticed me and he viciously slung his clawlike hand towards me and tried to slash me; but I jumped back. In an instant I was standing safely beside Jesus and watching the battle rage. Then Jesus ushered me over to a group of people behind the battle lines. I could see that they were praying, but there weren't many people. I saw an angel record what they were praying and then quickly ascend to the Father, and I heard the Father giving orders to send more angels into the battle. Next I noticed that the small group of people praying was now fewer in number and I began to cry. Then I was transported back into the thick of the battle being waged between Satan's demonic forces and God's angelic forces and I saw the angels binding the demons in chains as a result of the prayers.

Chapter Five

Mystery and Supernatural

Revelation 10:1–7

I saw still another mighty angel coming down from heaven, clothed with a cloud. And a rainbow was on his head, his face was like the sun, and his feet like pillars of fire. He had a little book open in his hand. And he set his right foot on the sea and his left foot on the land, and cried with a loud voice, as when a lion roars. When he cried out, seven thunders uttered their voices. Now when the seven thunders uttered their voices, I was about to write; but I heard a voice from heaven saying to me, "Seal up the things which the seven thunders uttered, and do not write them." The angel whom I saw standing on the sea and on the land raised up his hand to heaven and swore by Him who lives forever and ever, who created heaven and the things that are in it, the earth and the things that are in it, and the sea and the things that are in it, that there should be delay no longer, but in the days of the sounding of the seventh angel, when he is about to sound, the mystery of God would be finished, as He declared to His servants the prophets.

This massive angel planted his right foot on the sea and his left on the land and began to thunder out the contents of the little open book, but John was instructed not to write what he had heard. He was told that these sealed revelations would no longer be a mystery when the seventh trumpet was about to sound. Daniel was also told to seal up certain end times prophecies. "But you, Daniel, shut up the words, and seal the book until the time of the end; many shall run to and fro, and knowledge shall increase" (Daniel 12:4). God is a God who reveals, but certain end time revelations must remain a mystery to man until it is His set time for them to be understood. If God spelled out every detail for these end time events, man might try to circumvent those plans through the knowledge he has been given. God always gives His people just enough information to understand His plans. The Holy Spirit said this to me: "*I will show you more about the little book that you have rightly titled: "Mystery." To you, My child, I will show you the mysteries of the kingdom of God so that you may reveal them.*" "Let a man so consider us, as servants of Christ and stewards of the mysteries of God" (1 Corinthians 4:1). The Holy Spirit gave me a vision and this is what I saw. I saw the little book opened. Then I saw the shapes of countries rising up out of the book. By the outline of the shapes I could identify the various countries. First I saw the shape of Russia, then China, then Italy, then the United States, then France, then Germany, then Israel, and finally Great Britain. The Holy Spirit revealed to me that these countries will form an alliance when the end times are near, but the alliance will be short-lived. The break-up of this alliance will set the stage for the ten nations to align with the Antichrist. The book of Psalms tells of the conspiracy of these ten nations and how they will form an alliance with the Antichrist against Israel and Christ.

> For behold, Your enemies make a tumult;
> and those who hate You have lifted up their head.
> They have taken crafty counsel against Your people,
> and consulted together against Your sheltered ones.
> They have said, "Come, and let us cut them off from being a nation,
> that the name of Israel may be remembered no more."

> For they have consulted together with one consent; they form a confederacy against You.
> (Psalm 83:2-5)

The Holy Spirit explained this about what I saw in the Spirit. "*The little book that John was told to eat contains mysteries of these last days and I have shown you one of those mysteries. I know all things and I give details and information so My plans are fulfilled. Those details I give come about in a way that is not expected or can be reasoned in the mind; nonetheless, the events that I reveal will happen.*"

Revelation 10:8–11

> Then the voice which I heard from heaven spoke to me again and said, "Go, take the little book which is open in the hand of the angel who stands on the sea and on the earth." So I went to the angel and said to him, "Give me the little book." And he said to me, "Take and eat it; and it will make your stomach bitter, but it will be as sweet as honey in your mouth." Then I took the little book out of the angel's hand and ate it, and it was as sweet as honey in my mouth. But when I had eaten it, my stomach became bitter. And he said to me, "You must prophesy again about many peoples, nations, tongues, and kings."

John was told by the angel to eat the little book, and when he did it tasted sweet in his mouth but made his stomach upset. Ezekiel was also instructed by the Lord to eat a scroll that would be sweet to the taste but would result in bitter prophetic words to the house of Israel. "And He said to me, "Son of man, feed your belly, and fill your stomach with this scroll that I give you." So I ate, and it was in my mouth like honey in sweetness. Then He said to me: "Son of man, go to the house of Israel and speak with My words to them" (Ezekiel 3:3–4). These are the Lord's words to me regarding these Scriptures. "*John was instructed to eat the book because eating My Word brings life. I am the Resurrection and the Life. The book was sweet because it is My Word, but bitter because he was instructed to prophesy harsh words to nations, kings and peoples. A prophet's job is never easy and the rewards of a prophet are deferred until heaven. My true prophets speak My words regardless of the consequences. Throughout history, My prophets have been abused and suffered because they chose to listen to Me and then speak forth My word. I still communicate to My people today and reveal My plans. There are those who hear Me and are too fearful to speak and there are those who hear Me and lay fear aside and speak My words. My true prophets hear Me and then announce."*

Revelation 11:1–2

> "Then I was given a reed like a measuring rod. And the angel stood, saying, "Rise and measure the temple of God, the altar, and those who worship there. But leave out the court which is outside the temple, and do not measure it, for it has been given to the Gentiles. And they will tread the holy city underfoot for forty-two months."

John was told to measure the temple and the altar, but not the outer court. In the history of Israel, there have only been two temples that have existed on the Temple Mount in Jerusalem. Solomon's temple was destroyed by the Babylonians and Zerubbabel's temple that was expanded upon by Herod was destroyed by the Romans. There has not been a Jewish temple in Jerusalem since its destruction in A.D. 70, but there will come a time when the third temple will be built. Currently in Israel, there are small group of Jews that believe there will be a third temple built, and they have duplicated all the temple articles according to the description given in Exodus. They have made the table for the showbread, the gold lampstand, the altar for burnt offering, the altar of incense, the bronze lavers for washing, the holy anointing oil, the incense, musical instruments, and the silver trumpets. They have also very meticulously hand-made the high priest's garments which consist of the breastplate, ephod, robe, tunic, turban, and sash. These articles are on display at the Temple Institute in Jerusalem but the only piece they have not made is the ark of the covenant. They believe that right before the destruction of Solomon's temple in 586 B.C., the priests hid the ark in a secret cavern that was under the original temple. Temple worship cannot resume unless there is an ark, because this was the designated place that the manifest presence of God rested in the Old Testament. The ark was also where the high priest sprinkled the blood of the goat once a year to cover the sins of the people on the Day of Atonement. Currently, the Muslim temple occupies the Temple Mount, so no excavations can be done beneath the Temple Mount. Since most orthodox Jews are still looking for the Messiah to come, the restoration of their temple in Jerusalem would again establish the sacrificial system established by God in the Old Testament. It is apparent from Scripture that temple sacrifice will be reestablished by the Jews during the seven years of Tribulation. John had been told not to measure the outer court of this temple because it will be been overtaken by the Gentiles. This will occur at the three-and-a-half year mark of the seven years of Tribulation when the peace treaty with Israel has been broken. Isaiah prophesied that this covenant or peace treaty made by the Antichrist and Israel would be broken. "Your covenant with death will be annulled, and your agreement with Sheol will not stand; when the overflowing scourge passes through, then you will be trampled down by it" (Isaiah 28:18). It is very notable that Isaiah says in this Scripture that Israel made a covenant with death and hell when they agreed to this peace treaty with the Antichrist because they made a covenant with Satan. This is what the Lord revealed to me about this Scripture. *"The temple that John was told to measure will be the rebuilt temple in Jerusalem. This temple will be built on the Temple Mount because the earth will swallow the Dome and they will be fearful to rebuild on this sight. I will separate the earth and remove the temple of these heathens."* The largest fault line in the world called the Syria-Africa Fault Line runs the entire length of the country of Israel. Some experts believe it is just a matter of time before Israel has a major earthquake of catastrophic magnitude. God is sovereign, and with an earthquake He will be the One to reclaim His Temple Mount and remove the heathen. "The LORD is King for ever and ever: the heathen are perished out of his land" (Psalm 10:16 KJV).

REVELATION 11:3–14

> And I will give power to my two witnesses, and they will prophesy one thousand two hundred and sixty days, clothed in sackcloth." These are the two olive trees and the two lampstands standing before the God of the earth. And if anyone wants to harm them, fire proceeds from their mouth and devours their enemies. And if anyone wants to harm them, he must be killed in this manner. These have power to shut heaven, so that no rain falls in the days of their prophecy; and they have power over waters to turn them to blood, and to strike the earth with all plagues, as often as they desire. When they finish their testimony, the beast that ascends out of the bottomless pit will make war against them, overcome them, and kill them. And their dead bodies will lie in the street of the great city which spiritually is called Sodom and Egypt, where also our Lord was crucified. Then those from the peoples, tribes, tongues, and nations will see their dead bodies three-and-a-half days, and not allow their dead bodies to be put into graves. And those who dwell on the earth will rejoice over them, make merry, and send gifts to one another, because these two prophets tormented those who dwell on the earth. Now after the three-and-a-half days the breath of life from God entered them, and they stood on their feet, and great fear fell on those who saw them. And they heard a loud voice from heaven saying to them, "Come up here." And they ascended to heaven in a cloud, and their enemies saw them. In the same hour there was a great earthquake, and a tenth of the city fell. In the earthquake seven thousand people were killed, and the rest were afraid and

gave glory to the God of heaven. The second woe is past. Behold, the third woe is coming quickly.

There are two witnesses that prophesy in the Old City of Jerusalem for three-and–a-half years that have great power. Zechariah also prophesied about these two witnesses. "Then I answered and said to him, "What are these two olive trees—at the right of the lampstand and at its left?" And I further answered and said to him, "What are these two olive branches that drip into the receptacles of the two gold pipes from which the golden oil drains?" Then he answered me and said, "Do you not know what these are?" And I said, "No, my lord." So he said, "These are the two anointed ones, who stand beside the Lord of the whole earth" (Zechariah 4:11–14). In order to determine the identity of these two witnesses, one must first know that "it is appointed for men to die once" (Hebrew 9:27). According to the Word of God, there were only two prophets that never experienced death, but were taken to Paradise. Enoch and Elijah were both translated to heaven without experiencing a physical death on earth. These two prophets are God's appointed witnesses to come back to earth during the last three-and-a-half years of Tribulation. "And Enoch walked with God; and he was not, for God took him" (Genesis 5:24). "By faith Enoch was taken away so that he did not see death, 'and was not found, because God had taken him'; for before he was taken he had this testimony, that he pleased God" (Hebrews 11:5). "Then it happened, as they continued on and talked, that suddenly a chariot of fire appeared with horses of fire, and separated the two of them; and Elijah went up by a whirlwind into heaven" (2 Kings 2:11). "Behold, I will send you Elijah the prophet before the coming of the great and dreadful day of the LORD" (Malachi 4:5). The Lord explained these Scriptures. "*My two witnesses are indeed Elijah and Enoch. These two prophets did not taste death because I translated them to Paradise. They will prophesy after the peace treaty has been broken and I have given them great power. They will testify of My righteous anger and My wrath to come and they call people to repent of their sin. If anyone tries to harm them, My Word will proceed forth from their mouths and has the power to burn and devour with fire. I will give them power over the heavens, the water and the power to release any plague. Enoch and Elijah will prophesy and testify of the coming plagues and then the plagues will occur. When their task is complete, I will permit the Antichrist to kill them. Their dead bodies will lie in the street of Jerusalem and will not be given proper burials because the Antichrist has commanded them not to be buried. The people will celebrate, dance in the streets and give gifts to one another when they are killed. They think that once Enoch and Elijah are dead, then the plagues will stop. These events will be seen worldwide and while the cameras are on, Enoch and Elijah will rise from the dead and ascend to heaven. There will be an earthquake the same hour that Enoch and Elijah come up to heaven, and it will kill seven thousand in Jerusalem and one tenth of the buildings will collapse. There is one final plague that remains and is more horrific than all the others. With this final plague, I come immediately to smite the armies of the Antichrist."*

SEVENTH TRUMPET—REVELATION 11:15–19

Then the seventh angel sounded: And there were loud voices in heaven, saying, "The kingdoms of this world have become the kingdoms of our Lord and of His Christ, and He shall reign forever and ever!" And the twenty-four elders who sat before God on their thrones fell on their faces and worshiped God, saying:

"We give You thanks, O Lord God Almighty,
The One who is and who was and who is to come,
Because You have taken Your great power and reigned.
The nations were angry, and Your wrath has come,
And the time of the dead, that they should be judged,
And that You should reward Your servants the prophets and the saints,
And those who fear Your name, small and great,
And should destroy those who destroy the earth."

Then the temple of God was opened in heaven, and the ark of

His covenant was seen in His temple. And there were lightnings, noises, thunderings, an earthquake, and great hail.

SEVENTH BOWL—REVELATION 16:17–21

Then the seventh angel poured out his bowl into the air, and a loud voice came out of the temple of heaven, from the throne, saying, "It is done!" And there were noises and thunderings and lightnings; and there was a great earthquake, such a mighty and great earthquake as had not occurred since men were on the earth. Now the great city was divided into three parts, and the cities of the nations fell. And great Babylon was remembered before God, to give her the cup of the wine of the fierceness of His wrath. Then every island fled away, and the mountains were not found. And great hail from heaven fell upon men, each hailstone about the weight of a talent. Men blasphemed God because of the plague of the hail, since that plague was exceedingly great.

The Lord revealed to me about the seventh trumpet and bowl. *"This is My final plague before I come and judge the nations that have rebelled against Me. The loud voice that proclaims: "It is done" is the voice of God. It is His voice that activates the lightning, thunder, the tremendous earthquake and great hail."* When the Lord spoke this to me I was in awe. The exceedingly great voice of God the Father will cause this worldwide earthquake that flattens mountains and causes islands to be swallowed by the sea. His incredible voice will cause one-hundred-pound hailstones to plummet to the earth. The supremacy of His voice is amazing and awe inspiring! If His voice contains this much authority, then how powerful His fullness must be! It causes me to shudder in holy reverence of God. With three simple words—"It is done"—He changes the face of the earth with such dynamic force. Do we really know this God? Do we really understand our frailty compared to His omnipotence? Do we understand His great mercy in light of His magnificent power? Do we understand that we do not belong to ourselves but we belong to Him and He can do with us whatever He chooses? Do we understand that we are at His complete mercy? And wonderful is His mercy and love towards us! "*The great earthquake is one that is felt over the earth. It divides Jerusalem into three parts and causes buildings in cities worldwide to fall to the ground. Every island is swallowed up by the sea and every mountain is shaken and leveled. The fire and brimstone that has been reserved for Babylon will erupt and the entire city will be burned. She will never be inhabited again and no tree or plant will ever grow on the bed of asphalt that will remain. When the large hailstones hit the earth, they will cause the earth to rumble and anything in their path will be utterly destroyed.*" It is amazing that men will still blaspheme God when they know He has the power to utterly destroy them. In the book of Leviticus, the law required that blasphemers be stoned to death and in these end time days, blasphemers will be stoned from heaven with one–hundred-pound hailstones! "*There is a heavenly temple and it was after this temple that I had Moses fashion the earthly temple. The temple of God is opened so that all in heaven will see the ark of the covenant sprinkled with My blood.*

> But Christ came as High Priest of the good things to come, with the greater and more perfect tabernacle not made with hands, that is, not of this creation. Not with the blood of goats and calves, but with His own blood He entered the Most Holy Place once for all, having obtained eternal redemption. . . . Therefore it was necessary that the copies of the things in the heavens should be purified with these, but the heavenly things themselves with better sacrifices than these. For Christ has not entered the holy places made with hands, which are copies of the true, but into heaven itself, now to appear in the presence of God for us. (Hebrews 9:11–12, 23–24)

When My Father saw My blood, He pronounced His wrath upon men for slaying His Lamb. My final words when I hung the cross were, "It is finished." and

My Father's final words regarding the punishment of man will be, "It is done." My Father has final say when these events will come about. Only He knows the day and the hour I will return, but I have given you the signs that must first take place before I return. He who has an ear, let him hear what the Spirit says to the churches. When the abomination of desolation sets himself up as God in the temple, My time is at hand. This final plague is punishment for man's continual rejection of Me."

Chapter Six

The Deadly Trio

Revelation 12:1–6

> Now a great sign appeared in heaven: a woman clothed with the sun, with the moon under her feet, and on her head a garland of twelve stars. Then being with child, she cried out in labor and in pain to give birth. And another sign appeared in heaven: behold, a great, fiery red dragon having seven heads and ten horns, and seven diadems on his heads. His tail drew a third of the stars of heaven and threw them to the earth. And the dragon stood before the woman who was ready to give birth, to devour her Child as soon as it was born. She bore a male Child who was to rule all nations with a rod of iron. And her Child was caught up to God and His throne. Then the woman fled into the wilderness, where she has a place prepared by God, that they should feed her there one thousand two hundred and sixty days.

In these verses, a brief but very important history is given for Israel, Jesus, and Satan and how they are interrelated. Although the symbolism is not given directly to John regarding the woman, the child, the stars, and the fiery red dragon, previous Scriptures in the Bible make reference to who they are. The woman in these verses is Israel and the sun that she is clothed with is the Messiah coming from Israel. The moon under her feet shows that nations will bow to Israel's King and be under Him. The twelve stars around her head are the twelve angels of the twelve tribes that make up Israel. Joseph, who was a type of Christ, was also given a similar prophecy. "Then he dreamed still another dream and told it to his brothers, and said, "Look, I have dreamed another dream. And this time, the sun, the moon, and the eleven stars bowed down to me" (Genesis 37:9). The child in this entire Scripture is the Messiah, Jesus Christ. The fiery red dragon is Satan and the seven heads are seven world powers, the seven diadems are the seven rulers of these world powers, and the ten horns are the ten nations that join the Antichrist in the final Battle of Armageddon.

In this Scripture, Satan's original rebellion against God convinced one third of the angels to join him and they were cast to the earth.

> How you are fallen from heaven,
> O Lucifer, son of the morning!
> How you are cut down to the ground,
> You who weakened the nations!
> For you have said in your heart:
> "I will ascend into heaven,
> I will exalt my throne above the stars of God;
> I will also sit on the mount of the congregation
> On the farthest sides of the north;
> I will ascend above the heights of the clouds,
> I will be like the Most High"
> Yet you shall be brought down to Sheol,
> To the lowest depths of the Pit."
> (Isaiah 14:12–15)

Satan was cast to the earth at his fall, but Scriptures indicate that he still had access to heaven to make accusations against God's people.

> Now there was a day when the sons of God came to present themselves before the LORD, and Satan also came among them. And

> the LORD said to Satan, "From where do you come?" So Satan answered the LORD and said, "From going to and fro on the earth, and from walking back and forth on it." Then the LORD said to Satan, "Have you considered My servant Job, that there is none like him on the earth, a blameless and upright man, one who fears God and shuns evil?" So Satan answered the LORD and said, "Does Job fear God for nothing? Have You not made a hedge around him, around his household, and around all that he has on every side? You have blessed the work of his hands, and his possessions have increased in the land. But now, stretch out Your hand and touch all that he has, and he will surely curse You to Your face!" And the LORD said to Satan, "Behold, all that he has is in your power; only do not lay a hand on his person." So Satan went out from the presence of the LORD. (Job 1:6–12)

In this concise account of Revelation chapter twelve, Israel gave birth to Jesus and as soon as He was born, Satan placed it in the heart of Herod to kill this new King. But God intervened and an angel informed the wise men from the East to return by another route and warned Joseph to take the child and flee to Egypt. Every time that Satan devised a plan to thwart God's plan, it was foiled because the Lord is greater in power and wisdom. The history recorded in these verses has been fulfilled with the exception of two points. Israel has yet to flee into the wilderness to escape the Antichrist during the last three-and-a-half-years of the Tribulation, and Jesus has yet to rule the nations with a rod of iron because that will occur during His millennial reign on earth.

REVELATION 12:7–12

> And war broke out in heaven: Michael and his angels fought with the dragon; and the dragon and his angels fought, but they did not prevail, nor was a place found for them in heaven any longer. So the great dragon was cast out, that serpent of old, called the Devil

> and Satan, who deceives the whole world; he was cast to the earth, and his angels were cast out with him. Then I heard a loud voice saying in heaven, "Now salvation, and strength, and the kingdom of our God, and the power of His Christ have come, for the accuser of our brethren, who accused them before our God day and night, has been cast down. And they overcame him by the blood of the Lamb and by the word of their testimony, and they did not love their lives to the death. Therefore rejoice, O heavens, and you who dwell in them! Woe to the inhabitants of the earth and the sea! For the devil has come down to you, having great wrath, because he knows that he has a short time."

The war that John saw between Michael and the heavenly angels and Satan and his demons occurs at the midway point of Tribulation. Satan and his demons no longer are granted access to the heavens where he came to accuse the brethren. The reason that Satan no longer had access to go before God's throne to accuse the brethren on earth was because the brethren were no longer on earth. They had been taken up to heaven in the Rapture. So the great dragon called Satan is permanently cast to the earth and he makes his habitation in the sea. "In that day the LORD with His severe sword, great and strong, will punish Leviathan the fleeing serpent, Leviathan that twisted serpent; and He will slay the reptile that is in the sea" (Isaiah 27:1). Enraged that he is now confined to earth and the sea, Satan sets out to persecute Israel who gave birth to Jesus. When Satan realizes that he is now on a short chain and his power is limited to the earthly realm, his plan is to inhabit a person to do the greatest damage to Israel and the followers of Jesus Christ. It is Satan that places it within the heart of the individual to assassinate the Antichrist so that he can take over his body. It is one thing to be inhabited by a lesser demon that controls behavior, thoughts, emotions, words, and addictions, but quite another to be inhabited by Satan. The New Testament was full of people who were inhabited by demons and Jesus dealt with these unclean spirits by casting them out.

The man from Gadara was inhabited by a legion of demons so that chains and shackles could not contain him and also caused him to cut himself with stones. These demons begged Jesus to cast them into a herd of swine, and when the unclean spirits entered the pigs, two thousand ran over a cliff into the sea. Much of Jesus' earthly ministry was casting out unclean spirits. Some of these demons caused infirmities and some caused erratic and destructive behavior. Jesus cast a demon out of a mute man and he was able to speak. He rebuked the demon in a boy that had convulsions and foamed at the mouth and who was deaf and dumb. Once the demon was gone, the boy could hear, speak, and no longer had seizures. Jesus cast out an unclean spirit in a man in the synagogue in Capernaum. These types of demons still exist today and they do inhabit people and cause infirmities, diseases, and destructive behavior. The medical world has labeled them epilepsy, cancer, bipolar, schizophrenia, depression, and many more, when in reality there are spirits behind these maladies. Doctors can try and treat the symptoms, but unless the root cause is dealt with, there is no cure. It is only by the power of Jesus' name that these infirmities can be healed. Jesus' earthly ministry involved healing and casting out demons and He empowers His servants to do the same. Demons recognized and knew that Jesus was the Son of God because they were once angels in heaven before they joined Satan in his rebellion against God. Satan's rebellion against God will continue when he takes over the body of the Antichrist. The Antichrist had to be dead in order for Satan to completely inhabit his body because a Jew would never willingly agree to such an unholy union. In these last three-and-a-half years, Satan will lash out at the inhabitants of the earth through the Antichrist and do all he can to deceive many people. The only way that those remaining on the earth can overcome Satan and the Antichrist is by the blood of the Lamb and the word of their testimony. Many of those who come to Christ during the second half of the Tribulation will lose their lives but will gain eternal life. "For what will it profit a man if he gains the whole world, and loses his own soul?" (Mark 8:36). The Lord spoke these words to me. *"Child, there will be many who have lived with one foot in the world and one foot in a church that will not be taken up. They knew the truth of My Word, but refused to walk in My ways. Church attendance does not make one a child of God. The ways of the world are lying, theft, sexual immorality, idolatry, murder, unbelief, sorcery, and cowards who refuse to acknowledge Me as Lord. Some will repent of their sin during the Tribulation and truly become My followers. They will see much destruction and many will lose their lives because Satan will make war with them."*

REVELATION 12:13–17

> Now when the dragon saw that he had been cast to the earth, he persecuted the woman who gave birth to the male Child. But the woman was given two wings of a great eagle, that she might fly into the wilderness to her place, where she is nourished for a time and times and half a time, from the presence of the serpent. So the serpent spewed water out of his mouth like a flood after the woman, that he might cause her to be carried away by the flood. But the earth helped the woman, and the earth opened its mouth and swallowed up the flood which the dragon had spewed out of his mouth. And the dragon was enraged with the woman, and he went to make war with the rest of her offspring, who keep the commandments of God and have the testimony of Jesus Christ."

When Satan is cast to the earth, he will lash out at the Jews in Israel. But the 144,000 from the twelve tribes of Israel will miraculously escape into the wilderness where God nourishes and protects them from Satan during this last half of the Tribulation. This is what the Lord revealed to me: *"I will provide a way of escape for My remnant and keep them hidden and protected until My return. I have them hidden in caves and Satan will create a flood to try and kill them. But I will open up the earth with a quake that swallows up the flood waters. Satan is enraged that I have intervened and he will make war with those remaining in Jerusalem who belong to Me."*

Revelation 13:1–10

Then I stood on the sand of the sea. And I saw a beast rising up out of the sea, having seven heads and ten horns, and on his horns ten crowns, and on his heads a blasphemous name. Now the beast which I saw was like a leopard, his feet were like the feet of a bear, and his mouth like the mouth of a lion. The dragon gave him his power, his throne, and great authority. And I saw one of his heads as if it had been mortally wounded, and his deadly wound was healed. And all the world marveled and followed the beast. So they worshiped the dragon who gave authority to the beast; and they worshiped the beast, saying, "Who is like the beast? Who is able to make war with him?" And he was given a mouth speaking great things and blasphemies, and he was given authority to continue for forty-two months. Then he opened his mouth in blasphemy against God, to blaspheme His name, His tabernacle, and those who dwell in heaven. It was granted to him to make war with the saints and to overcome them. And authority was given him over every tribe, tongue, and nation. All who dwell on the earth will worship him, whose names have not been written in the Book of Life of the Lamb slain from the foundation of the world. If anyone has an ear, let him hear. He who leads into captivity shall go into captivity; he who kills with the sword must be killed with the sword. Here is the patience and the faith of the saints.

The Beast that John saw rising up out of the sea is the Antichrist. The seven heads are seven world powers and the ten horns with the ten crowns are the ten nations that align themselves with the Antichrist. Three Middle Eastern nations only join with the Antichrist through force because the Antichrist will conquer them.

Thus he said:
"The fourth beast shall be
A fourth kingdom on earth,
Which shall be different from all other kingdoms,
And shall devour the whole earth,
Trample it and break it in pieces.
The ten horns are ten kings
Who shall arise from this kingdom.
And another shall rise after them;
He shall be different from the first ones,
And shall subdue three kings.
He shall speak pompous words against the Most High,
Shall persecute the saints of the Most High,
And shall intend to change times and law.
Then the saints shall be given into his hand
For a time and times and half a time."
(Daniel 7:23–25)

The Antichrist is described as a combination of a lion, a bear, and a leopard. Daniel was also given a vision of these animals which represented the nations that would overtake Israel and become world powers.

And four great beasts came up from the sea, each different from the other. The first was like a lion, and had eagle's wings. I watched till its wings were plucked off; and it was lifted up from the earth and made to stand on two feet like a man, and a man's heart was given to it. And suddenly another beast, a second, like a bear. It was raised up on one side, and had three ribs in its mouth between its teeth. And they said thus to it: "Arise, devour much flesh!" After this I looked, and there was another, like a leopard, which had on its back four wings of a bird. The beast also had four heads, and dominion was given to it. After this I saw in the night

> visions, and behold, a fourth beast, dreadful and terrible, exceedingly strong. It had huge iron teeth; it was devouring, breaking in pieces, and trampling the residue with its feet. It was different from all the beasts that were before it, and it had ten horns. I was considering the horns, and there was another horn, a little one, coming up among them, before whom three of the first horns were plucked out by the roots. And there, in this horn, were eyes like the eyes of a man, and a mouth speaking pompous words. (Daniel 7:3–8)

The lion was the Babylonian rule through Nebuchadnezzar which was dominant like the king of the beasts and swift like an eagle. The bear was the Media-Persian rule and the three ribs seen in the bear's mouth were the nations of Babylon, Libya, and Egypt that were conquered by Cyrus with extreme cruelty. The leopard was the Grecian rule through Alexander the Great who conquered the known world with extreme rapidness, but his kingdom was divided among his four generals because of his untimely death. The next kingdom was the Roman Empire which was stronger than all the empires that preceded it. Out of the Roman dynasty would come ten horns or ten nations. The little horn is the Antichrist who will conquer three of the ten nations. The Antichrist will have the power and dominance of the Babylonians, the large number of troops as the Media-Persian reign, the swiftness of Alexander the Great, and the strength of the Roman Empire. Satan will give the Antichrist his power, his throne and authority when the Antichrist is mortally wounded by a sword, but is resurrected from the dead.

> Those who see you will gaze at you,
> And consider you, saying,
> "Is this the man who made the earth tremble,
> Who shook kingdoms,
> Who made the world as a wilderness

And destroyed its cities,
Who did not open the house of his prisoners?"
All the kings of the nations,
All of them, sleep in glory,
Everyone in his own house;
But you are cast out of your grave
Like an abominable branch,
Like the garment of those who are slain,
Thrust through with a sword,
Who go down to the stones of the pit,
Like a corpse trodden underfoot.
You will not be joined with them in burial,
Because you have destroyed your land
And slain your people.
(Isaiah 14:16–20)

It is the power of Satan that resurrects the Antichrist from the dead and Satan inhabits his body. As a result of the resurrected Antichrist, people will be amazed and worship him. People and nations will come to the conclusion that the Antichrist is immortal and therefore no one will be able to stop him through war. At the midway point of the Tribulation, the Antichrist that is indwelt by Satan will break the peace treaty with Israel. The Jews and the Christians in Israel will be the target of Satan's brutal attack because of his intense hatred of Jesus and the chosen Jewish nation that brought forth the Messiah. The Antichrist will openly blaspheme God and will have power to kill those saints who know Jesus Christ during the latter half of the Tribulation. This Tribulation period will be very vicious for the Jews and the Christians because Satan's vile anger towards God will be meted out upon the Olive Tree and the in grafted Wild Olive Tree. Those who survive the terror of the Antichrist will also experience the seven last plagues on earth because they did not embrace the gift of salvation through Jesus Christ before the Rapture.

If the sky rolled back like a scroll right now and Jesus appeared in the sky, would you be taken up to heaven? It is a question we all need to answer. If you are not sure, then it is because you have never asked Jesus to forgive your sins and become your Lord and Savior. The sin in your life separates you from God. Lying, stealing, cheating on your income taxes, having premarital sex, homosexuality, adultery, using God's name as a curse word, looking lustfully at woman or man, abortion, pornography, gluttony, losing your temper, are just a small list of many sins. The punishment for sin is condemnation to hell for all eternity where there is weeping and gnashing of teeth because of the constant torment. Hell is a real place prepared for people who have rejected Jesus Christ, just as heaven is a real place for those who have embraced Jesus Christ. You do have a body in hell along with all of your senses. You can see, touch, smell, hear, and thirst in hell. So imagine this scenario and you will get a graphic picture of hell. You have just died and been condemned to hell. You have been bound in leg irons and chains by an ugly hairy ape-like demon that has a hunched back, bulging eyes, crooked teeth, and a stench that almost makes you vomit. He forces you over to this earthen inferno that has raging flames spewing out, and just standing next to the opening begins to scorch your face and singe your hair. You can hear the agonizing screams of others that are being tortured in the distance, and you keep thinking that this is a horrible dream that you will awaken from at any moment, except you don't wake up. You are trembling at your treacherous fate, so much that you think you might just fall into this blazing hellhole from shaking so much. Then a pungent odor that is so horrific rises to your nostrils and you realize that it is the stench of burning flesh. Your mouth is so dry that it feels like your tongue has been dragged along the desert sand for days. Then without warning, this ugly evil creature lets out a hideous laugh as he pushes you bound into the flaming inferno. Every ounce of your flesh is being scorched all at the same time and the pain is excruciating. You can see your flesh melting and dripping from your body and you crave death to end this torture, but it eludes you. Then the maggots crawl all over your skeleton and you can feel their every move. Just when you think it is all over, the torture begins again with the flames scorching your body that somehow has its flesh restored, only to be burnt off once again. This is hell. It is a prepared place for people that have refused Jesus Christ's sacrifice on the cross as payment for their sin. Jesus Christ chose to be crucified on the cross for your sins, but the grave could not contain Him and on the third day He rose from that dead. Jesus is seated at the right hand of the Father and He will come to this earth a second time. The first time he came to be sacrificed as a Lamb, but the second time He will come as the Lion of Judah to rule the nations with an iron rod. If you confess your sins and ask Jesus to forgive you and believe in your heart that God raised Him from the dead, then you will be saved from the torments of hell. Heaven will then be your eternal destination. If you never had the opportunity to confess your sin and ask Jesus to be your Lord and Savior, then you are not saved. If you desire to make Jesus Christ your Lord and Savior, then make this declaration from your heart.

Jesus, I have sinned against You. (Right now, name and confess all your known sins to Jesus.) I choose to turn away from these sins that I have just spoken out loud and I ask You to forgive me. I believe that You were born of the Virgin Mary. I believe that You died on the cross to take away my sins, and I believe You rose from the dead on the third day. I believe that You are God and I receive You as My Lord and Savior, and I promise to love and obey You. Thank You, Jesus, for giving me eternal life in heaven. Thank You for writing my name in the Lamb's Book of Life because today I have become a child of God.

REVELATION 13:11–18

> Then I saw another beast coming up out of the earth, and he had two horns like a lamb and spoke like a dragon. And he exercises all the authority of the first beast in his presence, and causes the earth and those who dwell in it to worship the first beast, whose deadly wound was healed. He performs great signs, so that he

> even makes fire come down from heaven on the earth in the sight of men. And he deceives those who dwell on the earth by those signs which he was granted to do in the sight of the beast, telling those who dwell on the earth to make an image to the beast who was wounded by the sword and lived. He was granted power to give breath to the image of the beast, that the image of the beast should both speak and cause as many as would not worship the image of the beast to be killed. He causes all, both small and great, rich and poor, free and slave, to receive a mark on their right hand or on their foreheads, and that no one may buy or sell except one who has the mark of the name of the beast, or the number of his name. Here is wisdom. Let him who has understanding calculate the number of the beast, for it is the number of a man: His number is 666.

The second beast that will come from the earth will be a religious leader who will force people to worship the Antichrist. This religious leader is identified later as the False Prophet. These are the Lord's words to me: "*The false prophet will perform great signs and wonders to further deceive men. Those who don't know Me will be deceived by these signs and wonders; but those whose names that are written in the Lamb's Book of Life will not be deceived. The False Prophet will call down fire from heaven just like My prophet Elijah. He will cause the statue of the Antichrist to speak and will give power to the statue to kill anyone who will not bow down. At this crucial time, My saints must be patient and hold fast to their faith. It is the False Prophet who will require people to take the mark of the Beast on their right hands or foreheads. If a person does not have the mark, he cannot buy or sell. Microchips will be further developed and used as forms of identification for banking records, medical records, passports, driver's licenses and birth records. All who want to buy or sell will be required to have this chip implanted on either their right hands or foreheads. The chip is implanted at these locations because the skin is thin and the body will not reject the foreign object. I warn My people in advance not to take the mark of the Beast. Is it better to gain the world and lose your soul? Remember, I have repeatedly warned you that when the abomination of desolation is set up in the temple, My return is very close. Do not take the mark of the Beast. Do not bow down to the abomination of desolation that has set himself up as God. Do not love your life that you lose your eternal salvation. Do not fear death, but fear the One who can cast you into hell."* It is very profound that God told His people to bind His commandments as a sign on their hands and place them as frontlets between their eyes. The Antichrist and False Prophet chose the exact same location for their mark, which only exemplifies that Satan has no originality. He has a counterfeit evil plan that mimics God's original plan that is far superior.

The Antichrist has a number that is assigned to him and that number is 666. All throughout Scripture numbers are very significant and God includes them for a specific reason. God has not yet revealed how this number will be calculated, but in His perfect timing, God will reveal to those who are seeking His wisdom. This is what the Lord said to me: *"Child, I have hidden treasures of wisdom and knowledge in the numbers of Holy Scriptures. Numbers, hours, days, months, years and ages all have significance. Those who thirst after these hidden treasures, I will give great understanding. My Word is so full of hidden manna which is food for the spirit. He who is thirsty, come to the living waters and drink deeply and you will be satisfied."* During the Tribulation many will be deceived by the Antichrist's resurrection and the False Prophet's signs and wonders. Calculating this number may the only way that people will be able to determine that he is the true Antichrist. God will fill His people with a great spirit of wisdom and understanding to be able to calculate the Antichrist's number by what is revealed in Scripture. God is so full of mercy and love that He has written a very vivid description of the end times so that people will not be deceived.

Chapter Seven

Warning and Wrath

~

Revelation 14:1–5

Then I looked, and behold, a Lamb standing on Mount Zion, and with Him one hundred and forty-four thousand, having His Father's name written on their foreheads. And I heard a voice from heaven, like the voice of many waters, and like the voice of loud thunder. And I heard the sound of harpists playing their harps. They sang as it were a new song before the throne, before the four living creatures, and the elders; and no one could learn that song except the hundred and forty-four thousand who were redeemed from the earth. These are the ones who were not defiled with women, for they are virgins. These are the ones who follow the Lamb wherever He goes. These were redeemed from among men, being firstfruits to God and to the Lamb. And in their mouth was found no deceit, for they are without fault before the throne of God.

John saw Jesus Christ standing on Mount Zion in Jerusalem and surrounding Him were 144,000 Jews from the twelve tribes of Israel that were sealed, set apart, and protected during the Tribulation. The fact that John saw Jesus standing on Mount Zion shows that this event will take place during the millennial reign of Jesus on earth. These Jews, which are God's firstfruits, will sing a new song of victory and praise to Jesus that is unique and exclusive only to them. These 144,000 are redeemed, pure, chaste celibate men who have been set apart to Jesus and represent the nation of Israel. They are the first of the entire harvest of Israel, for when Jesus rules and reigns in Jerusalem for one thousand years, all of Israel will be saved. All of Israel will bow down to Jesus Christ and they will know that He is the Messiah. They will also mourn because they will understand that Israel rejected Jesus and crucified Him. "And I will pour on the house of David and on the inhabitants of Jerusalem the Spirit of grace and supplication; then they will look on Me whom they pierced. Yes, they will mourn for Him as one mourns for his only son, and grieve for Him as one grieves for a firstborn" (Zechariah 12:10). Once the mourning has passed, they will celebrate that their King is with them and their hearts will be filled with rejoicing.

REVELATION 14:6–13

> Then I saw another angel flying in the midst of heaven, having the everlasting gospel to preach to those who dwell on the earth— to every nation, tribe, tongue, and people— saying with a loud voice, "Fear God and give glory to Him, for the hour of His judgment has come; and worship Him who made heaven and earth, the sea and springs of water." And another angel followed, saying, "Babylon is fallen, is fallen, that great city, because she has made all nations drink of the wine of the wrath of her fornication." Then a third angel followed them, saying with a loud voice, "If anyone worships the beast and his image, and receives his mark on his forehead or on his hand, he himself shall also drink of the wine of the wrath of God, which is poured out full strength into the cup of His indignation. He shall be tormented with fire and brimstone in the presence of the holy angels and in the presence of the Lamb. And the smoke of their torment ascends forever and ever; and they have no rest day or night, who worship the beast and his image, and whoever receives the mark of his name." Here is the

> patience of the saints; here are those who keep the commandments of God and the faith of Jesus. Then I heard a voice from heaven saying to me, "Write: 'Blessed are the dead who die in the Lord from now on.'" "Yes," says the Spirit, "that they may rest from their labors, and their works follow them."

Each of these three angels makes very important proclamations to the inhabitants of the earth. Those who are on the earth at this time are either unbelievers or believers that have come to the saving knowledge of Jesus after the Rapture. God is so loving and full of great compassion that it is His desire that none should perish. Therefore He sends the first angel to proclaim the gospel with a loud voice to every nation, tribe, and tongue. This is God's final call for people to come to Christ and everyone on earth will hear it, so there will be no excuse for them when they stand before Christ to be judged. The second angel makes the proclamation that Babylon has fallen even before the event takes place. This prophetic announcement was given as a warning to the people who are residing in Babylon so they have an opportunity to leave Babylon, not only physically but also spiritually. God always gives plenty of warning before He pours out His wrath on man for sin. God's mercy and grace is abounding, but justice must prevail because He is a holy God and He will not tolerate sin indefinitely. Contrary to what some may think because they have a limited understanding of God, God does punish unrepentant people and unrepentant nations. Throughout the Old Testament, God told the Israelites that He would bless them abundantly if they kept the commands of the Lord, but He would curse them if they refused to obey the voice of the Lord. The blessings for obedience promised to the Israelites in the book of Deuteronomy covered every aspect of their lives. God would lavish His love upon them by multiplying their numbers, increasing their cattle, providing bountiful crops of grain and fruit by sending the necessary rain, removing all sickness and disease, healing all barrenness in both men and women, and delivering them victoriously over all the enemies of their land. God would spare nothing for them if they chose to obey Him and worship Him alone. The curse for their disobedience was fulfilled because the Israelites did not heed the voice of God and they indeed worshipped other gods. They were struck with diseases and plagues; the rain was scarce so their crops did not flourish; the locusts consumed much of their fields; they planted vineyards and olive trees only to be taken and consumed by other nations; they were defeated by their enemies and taken into captivity; and they would become few in number as the Lord scattered them among the nations. The Israelites refused to take heed to God's warning and they had to pay the penalty for their sin. God has also given the United States repeated warnings to turn from her sin, but our nation continues to ignore His warnings. Our country's forefathers were Bible reading, Christ believing founders who understood the utmost importance of acknowledging and obeying God. The religious freedom they desperately sought to protect was not so that everyone had a right to practice any religion, but so this nation could worship Jesus Christ without persecution. The United States of America has developed into a rebellious nation that would mortify our founding fathers. We kill millions of unborn babies, sexual sin is rampant, homosexuality is embraced as an alternate lifestyle, materialism is viewed as the all-American dream, money is elevated as god, and any mention of God is being removed from the land. God is patient and longsuffering, but at some point His justice must prevail. God is holy and He gets to choose how He punishes unrepentant sin, whether we acknowledge that it was His hand or not. As a result of our nation's sin, God lifted His hand of protection over the United States on September 11, 2001 when for the first time our homeland was attacked by terrorists. God judged our nation for turning our back on Him and embracing another god called money. The severe hurricanes that our nation has been pummeled with are also God's hand of judgment upon our nation for her sin. It is God who controls the wind, the rain and the oceans; it is not global warming as scientists suggest. There are blessings for hearing and obeying God and there are curses for disobedience. This choice is ours—do we choose blessings and life or cursing and death? "As it is written in the Law of Moses, all this disaster has come upon us; yet we have not made our prayer before the LORD our God, that we might turn from our iniquities and understand Your truth. Therefore the LORD has kept the disaster in mind, and brought it upon us; for the LORD our God is righteous in all the works which He does, though we have not obeyed His voice" (Daniel 9:13–14).

The third angel warned the people of the consequences of worshipping the beast and receiving his mark on their foreheads or right hands. Those who chose to worship the Antichrist will be tortured with fire and brimstone day and night for all eternity. These people that are tormented in pits of fire will be able to see Jesus and His angels, and their regret will be so intense because they will know they could have chosen Him. Instead of experiencing the everlasting joy of heaven, they will be in the terminal despair of hell where the torment never ends. Believers in Christ must be very patient and diligent not to permit fear to persuade them to take the mark of the Beast. The believers who lose their lives from this point forward will be blessed because they had to endure the final plagues and their dedication to the Lord Jesus will be severely tested.

REVELATION 14:14–20

> Then I looked, and behold, a white cloud, and on the cloud sat One like the Son of Man, having on His head a golden crown, and in His hand a sharp sickle. And another angel came out of the temple, crying with a loud voice to Him who sat on the cloud, "Thrust in Your sickle and reap, for the time has come for You to reap, for the harvest of the earth is ripe." So He who sat on the cloud thrust in His sickle on the earth, and the earth was reaped.
>
> Then another angel came out of the temple which is in heaven, he also having a sharp sickle. And another angel came out from the altar, who had power over fire, and he cried with a loud cry to him who had the sharp sickle, saying, "Thrust in your

> sharp sickle and gather the clusters of the vine of the earth, for her grapes are fully ripe." So the angel thrust his sickle into the earth and gathered the vine of the earth, and threw it into the great winepress of the wrath of God. And the winepress was trampled outside the city, and blood came out of the winepress, up to the horses' bridles, for one thousand six hundred furlongs.

There are two harvests that will be reaped from the earth. Jesus will reap the harvest of believers from the earth that belong to Him and an angel will reap the unbelievers and throw them into the winepress of God's wrath. Jesus expounded upon this final harvest when He explained the parable of the wheat and the tares to His disciples.

> Then Jesus sent the multitude away and went into the house. And His disciples came to Him, saying, "Explain to us the parable of the tares of the field." He answered and said to them: "He who sows the good seed is the Son of Man. The field is the world, the good seeds are the sons of the kingdom, but the tares are the sons of the wicked one. The enemy who sowed them is the devil, the harvest is the end of the age, and the reapers are the angels. Therefore as the tares are gathered and burned in the fire, so it will be at the end of this age. The Son of Man will send out His angels, and they will gather out of His kingdom all things that offend, and those who practice lawlessness, and will cast them into the furnace of fire. There will be wailing and gnashing of teeth. Then the righteous will shine forth as the sun in the kingdom of their Father. He who has ears to hear, let him hear! (Matthew 13:36–43)

The principle of sowing and reaping in the natural certainly applies to the spiritual realm. When a farmer sows a field of corn, he fully expects to reap a harvest of corn. If a person sows a life of rebellion against God, then he should fully expect to reap the consequences of destruction and devastation. Likewise if a person sows a life of obedience to God, then he will reap the benefits and blessings that accompany that life. "Do not be deceived, God is not mocked; for whatever a man sows, that he will also reap. For he who sows to his flesh will of the flesh reap corruption, but he who sows to the Spirit will of the Spirit reap everlasting life. And let us not grow weary while doing good, for in due season we shall reap if we do not lose heart. Therefore, as we have opportunity, let us do good to all, especially to those who are of the household of faith" (Galatians 6:7–10). The Lord explained this to me: *"John was witnessing the final harvest of the earth and the great winepress of God's wrath being poured out at the great Battle of Armageddon. Every person and animal that is gathered in the Jezreel Plain will be killed by the sword that comes out of My mouth. Blood will fill the plain up to the bridle of the horse."*

Chapter Eight

Fall of Babylon

The history and establishment of Babylon from its inception was founded on pride, rebellion, and idolatry. The same pattern of evil will occur in the end time Babylon, but only magnified. In order to establish the evil pattern of Babylon the Great in Revelation, the first mention of Babylon in Genesis must be examined.

> Now the whole earth had one language and one speech. And it came to pass, as they journeyed from the east, that they found a plain in the land of Shinar, and they dwelt there. Then they said to one another, "Come, let us make bricks and bake them thoroughly." They had brick for stone, and they had asphalt for mortar. And they said, "Come, let us build ourselves a city, and a tower whose top is in the heavens; let us make a name for ourselves, lest we be scattered abroad over the face of the whole earth." But the LORD came down to see the city and the tower which the sons of men had built. And the LORD said, "Indeed the people are one and they all have one language, and this is what they begin to do; now nothing that they propose to do will be withheld from them. Come, let Us go down and there confuse their language, that they may not understand one another's speech." So the LORD scattered them abroad from there over the face of all the earth, and they ceased building the city. Therefore its name is called

> Babel, because there the LORD confused the language of all the earth; and from there the LORD scattered them abroad over the face of all the earth. (Genesis 11:1–9)

After the flood when the sons of Noah began to repopulate the earth, they journeyed to the land of Shinar which is the ancient name of Babylon. This same city of Babylon is located in Iraq. The people of ancient Babylon became full of pride which can be seen in their desire to make for themselves a name. They were not satisfied with magnifying the name of God for delivering them from the wickedness of the world or thanking Him for His divine provisions for them. Instead they wanted to be elevated above the name and power of God by building a tower. They rebelled against God's instruction to fill the earth by building a city because they feared being scattered over the face of the earth. "Then God blessed them, and God said to them, "Be fruitful and multiply; fill the earth and subdue it" (Genesis 1:28). They committed idolatry by building a tower whose top was in heaven in a human effort to reach God. Instead of trusting in the name of the Lord to be their strong tower, they chose to build their own tower and trust in their own accomplishments. "The name of the LORD is a strong tower; the righteous run to it and are safe" (Proverbs 18:10). Any effort to reach heaven by good works or human efforts will fall short and the result will be eternal death. These ancient people had become so united among themselves that they were planning to eliminate God from their lives. Rebellion against God's Word to fill the earth and subdue it was temporarily circumvented by the people as they settled in the land of Babylon. But that wouldn't last for long, because God confused their language and they were forced to be scattered over the face of the earth. The same evil pattern that was birthed in the original Babylon will emerge for end time Babylon. There will be open rebellion against God, consuming pride, blatant idolatry based on a false world religion, and the uniting of the ten nations under the Antichrist in an attempt to overthrow the true Messiah, Jesus Christ.

REVELATION 17:1–7

Then one of the seven angels who had the seven bowls came and talked with me, saying to me, "Come, I will show you the judgment of the great harlot who sits on many waters, with whom the kings of the earth committed fornication, and the inhabitants of the earth were made drunk with the wine of her fornication." So he carried me away in the Spirit into the wilderness. And I saw a woman sitting on a scarlet beast which was full of names of blasphemy, having seven heads and ten horns. The woman was arrayed in purple and scarlet, and adorned with gold and precious stones and pearls, having in her hand a golden cup full of abominations and the filthiness of her fornication. And on her forehead a name was written: MYSTERY,

BABYLON THE GREAT,
THE MOTHER OF HARLOTS
AND OF THE ABOMINATIONS OF THE EARTH.

I saw the woman, drunk with the blood of the saints and with the blood of the martyrs of Jesus. And when I saw her, I marveled with great amazement. But the angel said to me, "Why did you marvel? I will tell you the mystery of the woman and of the beast that carries her, which has the seven heads and the ten horns."

The Harlot is Babylon and will be a powerful political and religious city of the false church. The many waters are peoples, multitudes, nations, and tongues that the harlot has influence over. The wine of fornication is false religion and deception, paired with evil doctrines and practices. This wine of fornication has already begun in the false church with the ordination of homosexual ministers, the marrying of homosexuals, and the promotion of abortion. This mother of harlots is seen sitting on a scarlet beast which is the Antichrist. Babylon will be the location where the Antichrist sets up his kingdom along with the False Prophet. The Harlot's apparel signifies her position of power as a leading world nation. Purple is the color of kingship and denotes Babylon's authority over the other nations, and scarlet corresponds to the shed blood of the saints because Babylon's religious system will not tolerate Christianity or Judaism. The gold, precious stones, and pearls show the wealth of Babylon during this time period and are a counterfeit of the heavenly city of the New Jerusalem. The city of Babylon will be Satan's answer to God's city of the New Jerusalem. In the hand of the Harlot is a golden cup of abominations which represents an evil communion table. The Apostle Paul warned the Corinthians about partaking of an evil communion table when he wrote: "You cannot drink the cup of the Lord and the cup of demons; you cannot partake of the Lord's table and of the table of demons" (1 Corinthians 10:21). The message that Paul was conveying to the church was that you cannot continually partake in sins of the world and partake of the Lord's communion table, for there is no communion with darkness and light. The true church cannot partake of practices of the world system and expect to have a relationship with the Lord. Babylon and everything that she represents will be a result of the influence of Satan. Therefore, practices that are truly evil will be called good and practices that are truly good will be called evil. Zechariah was also given a vision of a harlot inside a basket with a lead covering to contain her until the set time of God. This woman was carried by two angels to the land of Shinar. She is the same harlot of Babylon that was prophesied by John in the book of Revelation. Again, the Lord reveals important events in Scripture more than once to confirm His message to His people.

> Then the angel who talked with me came out and said to me, "Lift your eyes now, and see what this is that goes forth." So I asked, "What is it?" And he said, "It is a basket that is going forth." He also said, "This is their resemblance throughout the earth: here is

> a lead disc lifted up, and this is a woman sitting inside the basket"; then he said, "This is Wickedness!" And he thrust her down into the basket, and threw the lead cover over its mouth. Then I raised my eyes and looked, and there were two women, coming with the wind in their wings; for they had wings like the wings of a stork, and they lifted up the basket between earth and heaven. So I said to the angel who talked with me, "Where are they carrying the basket?" And he said to me, "To build a house for it in the land of Shinar; when it is ready, the basket will be set there on its base." (Zechariah 5:5–11)

REVELATION 17:7–11

> But the angel said to me, "Why did you marvel? I will tell you the mystery of the woman and of the beast that carries her, which has the seven heads and the ten horns. The beast that you saw was, and is not, and will ascend out of the bottomless pit and go to perdition. And those who dwell on the earth will marvel, whose names are not written in the Book of Life from the foundation of the world, when they see the beast that was, and is not, and yet is. "Here is the mind which has wisdom: The seven heads are seven mountains on which the woman sits. There are also seven kings. Five have fallen, one is, and the other has not yet come. And when he comes, he must continue a short time. And the beast that was, and is not, is himself also the eighth, and is of the seven, and is going to perdition."

There are more details given about the life of Antichrist in this chapter than any other in Revelation. The angel told John that the Antichrist was, and is not, and will ascend out of the bottomless pit and go to perdition. The Antichrist lives and then is killed by a sword, rises from the dead by the power of Satan, then will be thrown in the bottomless pit. At the three-and-a-half year mark of Tribulation, the Antichrist will be assassinated and then rise from the dead by the power of Satan. Satan will inhabit the body of the Antichrist at his resurrection. The unbelievers will marvel at this spectacular defeat of death and they will be convinced that the Antichrist is truly their Messiah. Initially, the Jews will be deceived because the Antichrist will be a Jew from the tribe of Dan and they had been looking for their Messiah to be an earthly king who would deliver them from the persecution of the surrounding nations. But when Satan enters the Antichrist and stops the temple worship and kills the Jews, they will know they made a covenant with death. Jesus predicted that His chosen people would not receive Him as Savior, but when one came in his own name they would receive him as their Messiah. "I have come in My Father's name, and you do not receive Me; if another comes in his own name, him you will receive" (John 5:43).

The angel also told John that there are seven kings, whereby five have fallen, one is, and the other has not yet come. I sought the Lord in prayer and this is what He revealed to me: *"Regarding these seven world leaders, five had already risen and fallen and one was in power when I gave My servant John these revelations. One more would come into power, but only for a short time. The Antichrist will be the eighth world ruler and he comes out of the seven world powers. These were kings that were types of the Antichrist and kings that directly adversely affected Israel."* After much research, these are the kings that follow the pattern and every one is a type of the Antichrist.

1. Nebuchadnezzar – Babylonian Empire
2. Alexander the Great – Grecian Empire
3. Antiochus Epiphanies IV – Assyrian Empire
4. Nero – Roman Empire
5. Titus – Roman Empire
6, Domitian- Roman ruler at the time of John's writing Revelation
7. Diocletian- Roman Empire
8. Anti- Christ- Jew from the tribe of Dan from the land of Syria

These brief descriptions of the activities of these kings will define them as types of the Antichrist. A type is a figure or representation of something or someone to come. These seven kings were a prophetic representation that would prefigure the Antichrist and their activities and character would paint a vivid picture of the future Antichrist.

1. Nebuchadnezzar set up a gold statue in Babylon and made a royal edict that when the sound of all kinds of music was heard, the people were required to fall down and worship the image. Those who refused to fall down and worship would be cast immediately into the fiery furnace. Nebuchadnezzar killed the Jews, took many into captivity, raped the land, destroyed the temple and pilfered the holy articles from the temple. The Antichrist will set up a statue in the temple in Jerusalem and will require people to bow down to his image and the penalty will be death for disobedience. He will kill the Jews when he breaks the peace treaty with them and he will rape the land.
2. Alexander the Great chose Babylon as his capital city. He conquered the known world with extreme rapidness and cruelty. To receive recognition as supreme ruler, he required provinces to worship him as God. He introduced a uniform currency system throughout the empire and promoted trade and commerce just as the Antichrist will do. He had an insatiable appetite for blood and massacred and enslaved thousands. Alexander's reputation preceded him, and when he came to Jerusalem to overtake her, Jerusalem opened her gates and welcomed him. Jerusalem will throw open her gates and also welcome the Antichrist when he signs a false peace treaty with her. Babylon will be the Antichrist's capital city.
3. Antiochus Epiphanies IV came out of the Grecian empire when the untimely death of Alexander the Great split his

kingdom among four generals. Syria was the nation of the north that Antiochus was ruler over. He was extremely cruel and his tax collectors massacred the Jewish people. In Jerusalem, he slaughtered a pig in the temple and sprinkled its blood in the Holy of Holies. He killed the high priest and put a stop to the daily sacrifices and set himself up as God. He stole the holy vessels, the golden altar, the table of show-bread, and the candelabrum. The Antichrist will also stop the daily sacrifices in the third Jewish temple and he will desecrate the temple by setting himself up as God. The Antichrist's extreme cruelty will be evidenced in the slaughter of the Jews and the Christians. Antiochus was from Syria and the Antichrist will also be from the land of Syria. In all of Scripture, Antiochus Epiphanies IV is the most complete picture of the Antichrist.

4. Nero was a Roman ruler from A.D. 54–68. He blamed the burning of Rome on Christians and viciously killed them. Some Christians were covered with the skins of wild beasts and then placed in an arena to be torn apart by wild dogs. Some were crucified while others were burned alive to be used as torches to light the night. A lot of scholars believe that Paul's trial was before Nero and he was beheaded in Rome. The Antichrist will severely persecute and kill Christians.
5. Titus was a Roman ruler who burned the temple in Jerusalem in A.D. 70, leaving only a portion of the western wall as a cruel reminder to the Jews of their loss. All who resisted were slaughtered. Sacrifices to pagan gods were made in the ruins of the temple court. This dark time in history for the Jewish people would scatter them all over the world, for they no longer had a temple or a nation to call their own. Titus also paraded his Jewish and Christian captives throughout the

region and threw them to the lions forcing them to fight gladiator style. Titus was dangerously like Nero in his charm, intellect, ruthlessness, and extravagance. He was gifted intellectually, was a gifted musician and was an excellent warrior. The Antichrist will also be very intellectual, have a charismatic charm; he will be an excellent war strategist and exert extreme cruelty.

6. Domitian was the cruel Roman ruler from A.D. 81–96 who exiled John to Patmos where the Book of Revelation was penned. Domitian commanded that all the lineage of David be put to death. He martyred the bishop of Jerusalem by crucifixion. It was a capital crime to be connected with the church and it was a custom to place an accused Christian to the test by requiring him to sacrifice to the image of the emperor. Like Nero, he was a bitter persecutor of the Christians. The churches in Asia Minor were in the midst of an awful and bloody persecution which resulted in the torture and death of multitudes of Christians. Domitian executed the Jews and the Christians that refused to worship the godhead of himself. He was the first of the emperors to deify himself during his lifetime by assuming the title of "Lord and God." The Antichrist will set himself up as God and will martyr many.
7. Diocletian was the king that was yet to come who would rule for a short time, and he is the final ruler that is very clearly a type of the Antichrist. He was a Roman ruler from A.D. 284–305. There were royal edicts published during his reign commanding Scriptures to be burned and those professing Christianity would be deprived of their liberty. The rulers of the church were put in prison. They could be set free if they sacrificed to the gods, but those who refused were tortured with countless tortures. There were multitudes of martyrs

throughout each province and this ten-year period was one of the most intense persecutions against Christians.

8. The Antichrist is the eighth king and comes out of one of the seven other kings. The Antichrist comes from the tribe of Dan and from the land of Syria. Syria was a country that was formed when Alexander the Great died at the age of thirty-two unexpectedly and the Grecian empire was divided among his four generals. Antiochus Epiphanies IV was ruler of Syria so the Antichrist does proceed out of the one of the seven kings. Another very interesting fact is that Golan Heights, which was formally controlled by Syria before the Six Day War in 1967, was the land given to the tribe of Dan. In Scripture, the land that is now called Golan Heights was called the land of Bashan and was given to the tribe of Dan by Joshua. "And of Dan he said: "Dan is a lion's whelp; he shall leap from Bashan" (Deuteronomy 33:22). It is not a coincidence that Syria has been demanding that Israel return the Golan Heights that she had occupied before the Six Day War of 1967. The Antichrist will be a Jew from the tribe of Dan and come from the land of Syria or land that Syria once controlled, possibly the Golan Heights.

REVELATION 17:12–18

The ten horns which you saw are ten kings who have received no kingdom as yet, but they receive authority for one hour as kings with the beast. These are of one mind, and they will give their power and authority to the beast. These will make war with the Lamb, and the Lamb will overcome them, for He is Lord of lords and King of kings; and those who are with Him are called, chosen, and faithful." Then he said to me, "The waters which you saw, where the harlot sits, are peoples, multitudes, nations, and tongues. And the ten horns which you saw on the beast, these

> will hate the harlot, make her desolate and naked, eat her flesh and burn her with fire. For God has put it into their hearts to fulfill His purpose, to be of one mind, and to give their kingdom to the beast, until the words of God are fulfilled. And the woman whom you saw is that great city which reigns over the kings of the earth.

These ten world leaders will align themselves with the Antichrist along with their armies in the final Battle of Armageddon. God placed it into the hearts of the ten nations to give their kingdoms to the Antichrist so that He could gather these rebellious nations for their punishment. The ten nations have a history of severe mistreatment of Israel and they will receive their punishment at the Battle of Armageddon. God does punish nations even years later for their mistreatment of His chosen people Israel. When Samuel was sent to anoint Saul as king, he gave Saul instructions to carry out God's punishment on the Amalekites for their mistreatment of Israel hundreds of years earlier when they came out of Egypt. "Thus says the LORD of hosts: 'I will punish Amalek for what he did to Israel, how he ambushed him on the way when he came up from Egypt. Now go and attack Amalek, and utterly destroy all that they have, and do not spare them. But kill both man and woman, infant and nursing child, ox and sheep, camel and donkey'" (1 Samuel 15:2–3). God's purpose in having the ten nations gather together in the Jezreel Plain is so that He can mete out His punishment on those nations that have tried to destroy Israel. These nations will try to overcome Christ who is the Lord of lords and King of kings and they will be utterly shocked when Christ appears in the sky with His army. The Lord spoke these words to me: *"In this final showdown, I will come back with My saints who have been called, chosen, and found faithful. Notice the progression—called, chosen, and faithful. First one must be called and then one must be chosen. Not all who are called are chosen for this great battle; only those who have been found faithful to the end. They will partake of this great battle where I have the victory over Satan, the Antichrist, the False Prophet, and those nations who joined them in the Valley of Jezreel. Gideon and his chosen army was a type of this great battle. With Gideon's army, 32,000 were called to the battle, but because of fear only 10,000 answered the call. This is the way it is with many I have called to serve Me. Many are called but only a fraction commit fully to My call and therefore they forfeit being chosen. Not all that are called into battle will go, only those I have divinely chosen. Only those men who I caused to lap up the water with their hands were chosen for Gideon's army so that they were further reduced from 10,000 to 300. I chose men who would be faithful and without fear who would follow the directions that I gave to Gideon. Anyone with rebellion or pride was dismissed from Gideon's army; for this victory had to be accomplished My way. It will be the same with My army of saints that I will choose to come back with Me for that great and awesome Battle of Armageddon. Many are called but few are chosen. Those who did not love their life and gave it up for Me and the sake of the gospel will be called and chosen. Those that have remained faithful to Me are My chosen servants."*

REVELATION 18:1–8

> After these things I saw another angel coming down from heaven, having great authority, and the earth was illuminated with his glory. And he cried mightily with a loud voice, saying, "Babylon the great is fallen, is fallen, and has become a dwelling place of demons, a prison for every foul spirit, and a cage for every unclean and hated bird! For all the nations have drunk of the wine of the wrath of her fornication, the kings of the earth have committed fornication with her, and the merchants of the earth have become rich through the abundance of her luxury." And I heard another voice from heaven saying, "Come out of her, my people, lest you share in her sins, and lest you receive of her plagues. For her sins have reached to heaven, and God has remembered her iniquities. Render to her just as she rendered to you, and repay her double according to her works; in the cup which she has mixed, mix double for her. In the measure that she glorified herself and lived lux-

> uriously, in the same measure give her torment and sorrow; for she says in her heart, 'I sit as queen, and am no widow, and will not see sorrow.' Therefore her plagues will come in one day—death and mourning and famine. And she will be utterly burned with fire, for strong is the Lord God who judges her.

There will be a mighty angel that proclaims that Babylon's future is one of total destruction. This angel will also warn God's people to get out of Babylon so they will not be recipients of God's anger and punishment that He will to bring upon the city because of their horrendous sin. Babylon's world commerce and trade will make her rich and the luxurious living will be shared by those nations who traded with her. Her iniquity of elevating money to the status of God will not go unpunished. Sexual immorality will be the accepted way of life for which Babylon will be utterly destroyed. Love for others will grow completely cold and the blood of the saints will be spilled in the streets. People will be desensitized to the cruelty and brutal murders. Sodom and Gomorrah were other cities in Scripture that foreshadowed the complete depravity of Babylon, and those cities were utterly destroyed by God. Two angels went to Sodom to warn Lot and his family to flee the city because God's wrath was about to descend. Lot, who was righteous, chose to live in an ungodly city, and there will be godly people who will choose to live in the ungodly city of Babylon. God will warn these people to flee Babylon because He is a God of mercy and judgment. The sins of Sodom and Gomorrah had reached heaven, and the sins of Babylon will reach heaven. "For we will destroy this place, because the outcry against them has grown great before the face of the LORD, and the LORD has sent us to destroy it" (Genesis 19:13). The Lord spoke this to me regarding the final demise of Babylon the Great. *"I have reserved a bed of burning tar and asphalt beneath the city that I will cause to erupt from beneath the earth's surface. In one day, Babylon will be utterly destroyed and she will never again be inhabited. The smoke from Babylon will rise up to My throne and her burning will appease My anger; for she deceived the nations."*

Revelation 18:9–24

The kings of the earth who committed fornication and lived luxuriously with her will weep and lament for her, when they see the smoke of her burning, standing at a distance for fear of her torment, saying, "Alas, alas, that great city Babylon, that mighty city! For in one hour your judgment has come." And the merchants of the earth will weep and mourn over her, for no one buys their merchandise anymore: merchandise of gold and silver, precious stones and pearls, fine linen and purple, silk and scarlet, every kind of citron wood, every kind of object of ivory, every kind of object of most precious wood, bronze, iron, and marble; and cinnamon and incense, fragrant oil and frankincense, wine and oil, fine flour and wheat, cattle and sheep, horses and chariots, and bodies and souls of men. The fruit that your soul longed for has gone from you, and all the things which are rich and splendid have gone from you, and you shall find them no more at all. The merchants of these things, who became rich by her, will stand at a distance for fear of her torment, weeping and wailing, and saying, "Alas, alas, that great city that was clothed in fine linen, purple, and scarlet, and adorned with gold and precious stones and pearls! For in one hour such great riches came to nothing." Every shipmaster, all who travel by ship, sailors, and as many as trade on the sea, stood at a distance and cried out when they saw the smoke of her burning, saying, "What is like this great city?" They threw dust on their heads and cried out, weeping and wailing, and saying, "Alas, alas, that great city, in which all who had ships on the sea became rich by her wealth! For in one hour she is made desolate." Rejoice over her, O heaven, and you holy apostles and prophets, for God has avenged you on her!

Then a mighty angel took up a stone like a great millstone and threw it into the sea, saying, "Thus with violence the great

> city Babylon shall be thrown down, and shall not be found anymore. The sound of harpists, musicians, flutists, and trumpeters shall not be heard in you anymore. No craftsman of any craft shall be found in you anymore, and the sound of a millstone shall not be heard in you anymore. The light of a lamp shall not shine in you anymore, and the voice of bridegroom and bride shall not be heard in you anymore. For your merchants were the great men of the earth, for by your sorcery all the nations were deceived. And in her was found the blood of prophets and saints, and of all who were slain on the earth.

The nations that prospered greatly by partaking of the buying, selling and trading with Babylon will be in absolute shock when the news of her total destruction reaches them. These nations will lament because their source of luxurious living has been completely cut off. There will be no rescue efforts because the entire city will be burnt and the hot tar and asphalt will remain burning for days and will prevent people from coming near. People will be too fearful to get near the burning rubble and hot ash of Babylon. Ships will remain in port and witness the smoke rising from the city and bemoan their lost profits. Although the world will be lamenting the loss of Babylon, the prophets and apostles will be rejoicing in heaven because God has avenged their blood. Babylon will never again be an inhabitable city and her demise will be final. She has been judged by God for slaughtering the prophets and saints and deceiving the nations with her sorcery. Babylon, the headquarters of the Antichrist, who instituted the one world government and the one world religion, will be totally destroyed by God.

Chapter Nine

Victory of Christ

Revelation 19:1–10

After these things I heard a loud voice of a great multitude in heaven, saying, "Alleluia! Salvation and glory and honor and power belong to the Lord our God! For true and righteous are His judgments, because He has judged the great harlot who corrupted the earth with her fornication; and He has avenged on her the blood of His servants shed by her." Again they said, "Alleluia! Her smoke rises up forever and ever!" And the twenty-four elders and the four living creatures fell down and worshiped God who sat on the throne, saying, "Amen! Alleluia!" Then a voice came from the throne, saying, "Praise our God, all you His servants and those who fear Him, both small and great!" And I heard, as it were, the voice of a great multitude, as the sound of many waters and as the sound of mighty thunderings, saying, "Alleluia! For the Lord God Omnipotent reigns! Let us be glad and rejoice and give Him glory, for the marriage of the Lamb has come, and His wife has made herself ready." And to her it was granted to be arrayed in fine linen, clean and bright, for the fine linen is the righteous acts of the saints. Then he said to me, "Write: 'Blessed are those who are called to the marriage supper of the Lamb!'" And he said to me, "These are the true sayings of God." And I fell at his feet to worship him. But he said to me, "See that you do not do that! I

> am your fellow servant, and of your brethren who have the testimony of Jesus. Worship God! For the testimony of Jesus is the spirit of prophecy."

All of heaven praises and worships the Lord God for judging Babylon because the blood of the saints and the prophets has been avenged. Jeremiah prophesied about the final fall of Babylon and the accompanying rejoicing. "Therefore behold, the days are coming that I will bring judgment on the carved images of Babylon; her whole land shall be ashamed, and all her slain shall fall in her midst. Then the heavens and the earth and all that is in them shall sing joyously over Babylon; for the plunderers shall come to her from the north," says the LORD. As Babylon has caused the slain of Israel to fall, so at Babylon the slain of all the earth shall fall" (Jeremiah 51:47-49).

Before Jesus returns to rule and reign on earth there will be a marriage supper of the Lamb in heaven with His bride, the church. The Holy Spirit spoke these words to me comparing an earthly marriage between a man and woman and the marriage of the bride to Christ. *"Child, the marriage between a man and a woman is a picture of Christ and the church. Jesus will provide, protect, and possess His bride and in turn He wants His bride to serve, be sensitive, and submit to Him. These qualities that pertain to the marriage of the Lamb to His bride also pertain to an earthly marriage between a man and a woman. I have given the man inherent qualities to provide, protect, and possess the woman he loves and takes as his wife. I have given the woman inherent qualities to serve, be sensitive, and submit to the man she loves and takes as her husband.*

> Wives, submit to your own husbands, as to the Lord. For the husband is head of the wife, as also Christ is head of the church; and He is the Savior of the body. Therefore, just as the church is subject to Christ, so let the wives be to their own husbands in everything. Husbands, love your wives, just as Christ also loved the church and gave Himself for her, that He might sanctify and

> cleanse her with the washing of water by the word, that He might present her to Himself a glorious church, not having spot or wrinkle or any such thing, but that she should be holy and without blemish. So husbands ought to love their own wives as their own bodies; he who loves his wife loves himself. For no one ever hated his own flesh, but nourishes and cherishes it, just as the Lord does the church. (Ephesians 5:22–29)

The inherent qualities that God has given both the man and the woman are displayed in a godly marriage in this manner. The husband provides for his wife and in turn she serves him. A godly man will provide income for his wife and family and a godly wife serves her husband by taking care of the home and providing the meals. Both are equally important in marriage and both identify the man as the provider and the woman as the server. A man's identity is wrapped up in his ability to provide and that is why most men are so driven to work and make money. When a man is unemployed, his self-worth is depleted because the inherent quality to provide has been removed. A woman's identity is often connected to the home that she cares for and the children she nurtures and loves. Most women receive gratification and take pleasure in their homes and for that reason they decorate, improve, and keep a clean home. By providing a well-kept home she is conveying to her husband that she loves and cares for him, and by cooking his meals she shows her appreciation for his provisions for her. To some this may sound old-fashioned, so I suggest you take up your complaint with the Lord because He is the One who has given both man and woman these inborn traits. A man's instinct tells him to protect and watch over his wife and family and he was created bigger and stronger than the woman for this reason. Men are fascinated and drawn to weaponry because of his inherent quality to protect. Ultimately, the motivation behind a man going to war is to protect his wife and family from an enemy. One of the greatest ways a man can protect his family from an enemy is by taking the role of the spiritual leader of his home. Only a man of God who loves Christ with all his heart, soul, and strength can love his wife unconditionally and fully protect her from the unseen enemy who walks around like a roaring lion seeking to devour. The complement to man's ability to protect is the woman's sensitive nature to nurture, care, and be tender. The sensitive part of a woman allows her to respond in love to her husband's protection and it also equips her to nurture and care for her children. The wife's sensitivity to the husband's spiritual headship for her protection is imperative. When she comes under his protection as the spiritual leader, the entire family is secure, which satisfies her need to see her children nurtured in a safe environment. The man also has a desire to possess his woman whereby he says through the wedding ring, "You are mine and no other man shall have you." This is where protection will arise within a man if he notices another man paying undue attention to his wife. He will abruptly remove his wife from the other man and let her know in no uncertain terms that she belongs to him. Deep down a woman wants to be so desired by her husband in this manner that she willingly submits to his possession of her. A woman desires a knight in shining armor who swoops her up onto that white horse, wraps his arms around her and whispers in her ear: "You are mine alone." There is an inherent desire built within her to submit to her husband's complete possession of her that fulfills her need for love. The complementing qualities of a man to possess his wife and the woman's desire to submit to her husband stir the passion that is needed for a husband and wife to become one. Jesus spoke this to me: *"That is the mystery that I spoke of through My servant Paul. A man will leave his parents and cleave to his wife and they become one. So it is with Me and My church. I left My Heavenly Father to cleave to My bride to become one with her. When a husband and wife come together, they make a new creation and a child is born. When I come together with My church, a new creation is made and a child of God is born by My Spirit. You must be born of the water and the Spirit. The natural birth is by the water and the rebirth is by the Spirit. Only those who are born of the water and the Spirit can enter into the kingdom of God. Now you can see why Satan has attacked the marriage so vehemently and kills the unborn babies. Both are a picture of the kingdom of God. Unless one is born of the water and by My Spirit, one cannot enter My kingdom. I created a husband to protect, provide, and possess his wife. I created a wife to serve, to be sensitive and to submit to her husband. This models the marriage of the Lamb to His bride. I, Jesus Christ, promise to provide, protect, and possess My church. I expect My church to serve, to be sensitive, and to submit to Me. All who partake of the wedding supper of the Lamb are My bride. There is a great banquet in heaven before I return to earth to rule and reign in Jerusalem. Everyone whose name is written in the Lamb's Book of Life is invited to this great banquet to celebrate the marriage of the Lamb to His bride."*

REVELATION 19:11–21

> Now I saw heaven opened, and behold, a white horse. And He who sat on him was called Faithful and True, and in righteousness He judges and makes war. His eyes were like a flame of fire, and on His head were many crowns. He had a name written that no one knew except Himself. He was clothed with a robe dipped in blood, and His name is called The Word of God. And the armies in heaven, clothed in fine linen, white and clean, followed Him on white horses. Now out of His mouth goes a sharp sword, that with it He should strike the nations. And He Himself will rule them with a rod of iron. He Himself treads the winepress of the fierceness and wrath of Almighty God. And He has on His robe and on His thigh a name written: KING OF KINGS AND LORD OF LORDS. Then I saw an angel standing in the sun; and he cried with a loud voice, saying to all the birds that fly in the midst of heaven, "Come and gather together for the supper of the great God, that you may eat the flesh of kings, the flesh of captains, the flesh of mighty men, the flesh of horses and of those who sit on them, and the flesh of all people, free and slave, both small and great." And I saw the beast, the kings of the earth, and their armies, gathered together to make war against Him who sat on the

> horse and against His army. Then the beast was captured, and with him the false prophet who worked signs in his presence, by which he deceived those who received the mark of the beast and those who worshiped his image. These two were cast alive into the lake of fire burning with brimstone. And the rest were killed with the sword which proceeded from the mouth of Him who sat on the horse. And all the birds were filled with their flesh.

Jesus Christ is mounted on a gorgeous white stallion robed in complete majesty ready to make war and judge the rebellious people of the earth. Riding on white horses behind the Lord of lords and King of kings are the righteous saints of heaven. Although Jesus Christ could have easily conquered the 200 million men gathered in Megiddo by Himself, He will bring the saints of heaven to this great battle so they can share in the victory. The prophet Joel foretold of this great day of the Lord coming with His saints.

> The earth quakes before them,
> The heavens tremble;
> The sun and moon grow dark,
> And the stars diminish their brightness.
> The LORD gives voice before His army,
> For His camp is very great;
> For strong is the One who executes His word.
> For the day of the LORD is great and very terrible;
> Who can endure it?
> (Joel 2:10–11)

Joel said that the "LORD gives voice before His army" and John states that "out of His mouth goes a sharp sword, that with it He should strike the nations." The spoken word that proceeds out of the mouth of Jesus will pronounce judgment and annihilate this rebellious army, and Zechariah painted a very graphic picture of this final battle of Armageddon.

> Then the LORD will go forth and fight against those nations, as He fights in the day of battle. And in that day His feet will stand on the Mount of Olives, which faces Jerusalem on the east. And the Mount of Olives shall be split in two, from east to west, making a very large valley; half of the mountain shall move toward the north and half of it toward the south. Then you shall flee through My mountain valley, for the mountain valley shall reach to Azal. Yes, you shall flee as you fled from the earthquake in the days of Uzziah king of Judah. Thus the LORD my God will come, and all the saints with You. It shall come to pass in that day that there will be no light; the lights will diminish. It shall be one day which is known to the LORD— neither day nor night. But at evening time it shall happen that it will be light. And this shall be the plague with which the LORD will strike all the people who fought against Jerusalem: their flesh shall dissolve while they stand on their feet, their eyes shall dissolve in their sockets, and their tongues shall dissolve in their mouths. It shall come to pass in that day that a great panic from the LORD will be among them. Everyone will seize the hand of his neighbor, and raise his hand against his neighbor's hand; Judah also will fight at Jerusalem. And the wealth of all the surrounding nations shall be gathered together: gold, silver, and apparel in great abundance. Such also shall be the plague on the horse and the mule, on the camel and the donkey, and on all the cattle that will be in those camps. So shall this plague be. (Zechariah 14:3–7, 12–15)

According to these Scriptures, the Lord Jesus will come back and plant His feet on the Mount of Olives, the same place where He ascended to heaven. The Mount of Olives will split in two from east to west, leaving a large valley that will permit those held in captivity in Jerusalem to escape. This fissure that will split the Mount of Olives in two will continue down the Mount through the Garden of Gethsemane, through the Kidron Valley until it splits open the sealed Eastern Gate of Jerusalem. When I was in Israel standing in front of the Church of All Nations that is next to the Garden of Gethsemane, I was facing the sealed Eastern Gate. While praying in tongues, the Spirit of God showed me the great fissure that will occur when Jesus plants His feet on the Mount of Olives. The Spirit showed me that Jesus will not enter in the current Eastern Gate of Jerusalem that is walled off, but He will enter through the original Eastern Gate that is buried beneath. This large cleft will expose the Old Eastern Gate, and the Spirit showed me what it looked like. The current Eastern Gate is made of large white limestone that is evenly cut, but the old Eastern Gate I saw had rounded stones that were dark in color. Jesus will enter this Eastern Gate and lead those captive in Jerusalem to safety. Then Jesus will focus His attention on the army gathered in the Jezreel Plain. This 200 million man army will see Jesus on His white horse and they will be filled with fear and regret because they will know that they have been deceived, but it is too late. In those moments before their total destruction, they will know that their course has been set by their own decision to follow the Antichrist and the False Prophet. They will know that the true Messiah is before them and that He is the Lord of lords and King of kings. There is nowhere to hide from the wrath of God and their fate has been sealed. The spoken word that proceeds out of the mouth of Jesus Christ will pronounce judgment and this rebellious army will be desecrated by the Word of God. Their flesh will melt from their faces and their eyes and tongues will literally disintegrate. The carnivorous birds that have been summoned by the angel will feast on the carcasses of these rebellious men of war who rejected God. The blood from this great battle will cover the Jezreel Plain. The Antichrist and the False Prophet will be captured and thrown alive into the lake of fire burning with brimstone.

While worshipping the Lord one morning, He gave me a second vision of this final Battle of Armageddon and this is what I saw. I saw Jesus on a large white horse, but I did not see His face because He was not facing me. The robe that He was wearing was the most magnificent blue and it was long and draped over the flanks of the horse. Behind Jesus, filling the entire sky were people on white horses and in their hands were gold trumpets. Then I saw the Megiddo Plain filled with the massive army. They all looked up and saw Jesus in the heavens and immediately tremendous fear washed over their faces. These armed men dropped their weapons, and I saw some frantically trying to run away. Then I witnessed the most horrific scene I have ever viewed. The Lord showed me the face of one man receiving the judgment of Jesus Christ at this final Battle of Armageddon. Terrifying fear and great remorse washed over the face of this young soldier as his gaze was fixed on Jesus. Then I saw his eyes begin to protrude out of his sockets. His eyes bulged and enlarged until they became red and bloody and then they just exploded into a gory mess. Then I saw the skin on his face melt off until there was only a skull that remained. I was sobbing uncontrollably because of the graphic and horrific scene that I saw in this vision. I was on my knees with my face to the floor, and through my deep wrenching sob the Lord said to me: *"I will show you no more, for that is all you can handle."* Still sobbing and shaking the Lord said to me: *"Be still, child."* With these three words, He instantly calmed me, and all of the terror of the scene that I had witnessed was gone.

The Holy Word of God is truth and within the pages of God's written Word are countless treasures that reveal His plan. God gave His church great insights through His prophets in the Old Testament that gave vital information about the coming Messiah. There are three hundred, thirty-two prophecies that were foretold about Jesus' birth, life, death, burial, and resurrection that have already been fulfilled. There are also Scriptures that foretell the second coming of Jesus Christ and events that must take place first before He comes. The temple in Jerusalem must first be rebuilt, there must be a Middle Eastern peace treaty for Israel, the daily sacrifices will be taken away by the Antichrist, and the temple will be desecrated when a statue of the Antichrist is set up in the temple and worshipped as God. We have not witnessed any such events yet, but Scriptures do provide great insight as to the time frame when these will occur. Examining the original feasts of Israel will produce a fuller understanding about the revelations of Jesus' second coming.

In the Old Testament, God gave the Israelites three major feasts they were required to celebrate: The Feast of Passover, the Feast of Pentecost and the Feast of Tabernacles. The Feast of Passover had three parts that were celebrated: the Feast of Passover, the Feast of Unleavened Bread, and the Feast Day of the Sheaf of Firstfruits. The Feast of Passover was the remembrance of the death angel passing over the Israelites in Egypt before their Exodus. A lamb without spot or blemish was set aside ten days before and on the fourteenth day the Israelites were instructed to kill the lamb, place the blood on the doorposts and the lintel, and roast the lamb. When the angel of death killed the firstborn that did not have the blood of the lamb on the doorposts and lintels, the Egyptians gladly let the Israelites leave. The Israelites left Egypt with all their possessions, family, livestock and many precious items given to them by the Egyptians. The Passover has been fulfilled by Jesus Christ when He became the Lamb of God to take away all the sin of the world and conquer death by rising from the dead. Jesus' death and resurrection allow the believer to pass from death to life through faith in Jesus' sacrificial blood. The Lord Jesus instituted the ordinance of Communion as a remembrance of His death and resurrection, just as God established the Passover as a remembrance from the deliverance from death. Another part of this feast was the Feast of Unleavened Bread. For the seven days beginning at Passover, the Jewish house could contain no leaven and the entire household ate unleavened bread. They gathered all the leaven and anything that contained yeast and removed it from their homes and burnt it. The unleavened bread represented that Israel was about to be separated from the life of slavery and bondage in Egypt and their exodus would be made in haste. The fulfillment of the Feast of Unleavened Bread is the consecration and separation of the believer to the Lord because he is set free from the bondage of sin. The final part of the Passover was the Feast day of the Sheaf of Firstfruits. When Israel entered into the Promised Land, they were commanded to keep this feast day. The feast involved the harvest therefore it was not kept in the wilderness because God fed them with manna from heaven. The feast was carried out in this manner. A person would go to the ripened harvest of barley and wheat and cut one sheaf and bring it to the priest. The priest took this lone sheaf and waved it before the Lord in His house which was a thanksgiving for the coming harvest. This first sheaf represented the firstfruits of the harvest, and Israel was very familiar with the importance of this concept because of the importance of the firstborn. The firstfruits or firstborn were always holy to the Lord. The fulfillment of this feast is the person of Jesus Christ because His resurrection represented the great harvest of resurrected people yet to come.

The feast of Pentecost stood as a feast by itself. In the third month when the children of Israel were given the Ten Commandments, they experienced the Feast of Pentecost. This was also the time when the tabernacle of the Lord, the priesthood, and sacrificial system were given to the nation. The Jewish people today look upon the Feast of Pentecost as the celebration or commemoration of the giving of the law. From the Feast of Passover on the fourteenth day of the first month to the Feast of Pentecost was fifty days. The fulfillment of this feast occurred when the Holy Spirit was poured out upon the waiting disciples of Jesus Christ, fifty days after Jesus' resurrection during the feast of Pentecost in Jerusalem.

The Feast of Tabernacles is the third feast and also contains three feasts. The Blowing of the Trumpets was on the first day of the seventh month and was the distinct call to the great Day of Atonement, followed by the Feast of Tabernacles. This seventh month was ushered in by the trumpets, but with a special emphasis. The trumpet call and message was distinct in that it was a call to all Israelites to come to the sanctuary for the solemn Day of Atonement. The Day of Atonement was the most solemn day of all the feasts because it was a day of national cleansing and a cleansing of the sanctuary. This day only took place one day a year when the high priest entered into the Holy of Holies with the blood of a goat. He sprinkled the mercy seat of the ark with the blood of the sin offering which brought about the cleansing of all sin, iniquity, and transgression. The Day of Atonement was fulfilled by Jesus Christ when He took His blood and sprinkled the heavenly ark with His shed blood, signifying that sins were now forgiven and removed, not just covered. The Feast of the Blowing of the Trumpets has its fulfillment as the church sounds forth as a trumpet the gospel message of Jesus Christ. This feast will have its complete fulfillment when the seventh trumpet is sounded which will usher in the second coming of Jesus Christ.

The Feast of Tabernacles was to commemorate Israel's first encampment after their exodus from Egypt. The booths that they set up for this feast spoke of the temporary dwelling place that they had before entering into the Promised Land. This feast also coincided with the final harvest of the year, which was the ingathering of the fruit at the end of the year. In all the feasts of Israel, this one has not yet found its fulfillment with Christ or the church. The church has not yet seen the final harvest of souls and Christ has not yet returned to tabernacle with His people. The believer in Christ is also reminded that the earthly physical body is only a temporary tabernacle and that one day he will have an immortalized glorified body. The fullness of this Feast of Tabernacles will be experienced at the second coming of Christ and the resurrection of all the saints. The Feast of Tabernacles is the only feast that is mentioned in Scripture that will be celebrated by the nations in Jerusalem during the millennial reign of Jesus Christ.

> And it shall come to pass that everyone who is left of all the nations which came against Jerusalem shall go up from year to year to worship the King, the LORD of hosts, and to keep the Feast of Tabernacles. And it shall be that whichever of the families of the earth do not come up to Jerusalem to worship the King, the LORD of hosts, on them there will be no rain. If the family of Egypt will not come up and enter in, they shall have no rain; they shall receive the plague with which the LORD strikes the nations

> who do not come up to keep the Feast of Tabernacles. This shall be the punishment of Egypt and the punishment of all the nations that do not come up to keep the Feast of Tabernacles. In that day "HOLINESS TO THE LORD" shall be engraved on the bells of the horses. The pots in the LORD's house shall be like the bowls before the altar. Yes, every pot in Jerusalem and Judah shall be holiness to the LORD of hosts. Everyone who sacrifices shall come and take them and cook in them. In that day there shall no longer be a Canaanite in the house of the LORD of hosts. (Zechariah 14:16–21)

The Holy Spirit did a wonderful work in opening up the eyes of my understanding regarding the Feast of Tabernacles. In light of the fact that the Feast of Tabernacles is the only feast that has not found its complete fulfillment in Christ or the church, the Lord wanted to reveal its significance so that we could better understand the timetable of His second coming. There were prescribed animal sacrifices on set days for the original Feast of Tabernacles. Taken from Numbers Chapter 29, the following chart can be made regarding the sacrifices required for each day for the Feast of Tabernacles.

FEAST OF TABERNACLES
Numbers 29

	Bulls	Rams	Lambs	
Day 1	13	2	14	14 generations from Abraham to David
Day 2	12	2	14	14 generations from David to Captivity
Day 3	11	2	14	14 generations from Captivity to Christ
Day 4	10	2	14	14 generations of the Church Age
Day 5	9	2	14	14 generations of the Church Age
Day 6	8	2	14	14 generations of the Church Age
Day 7	7	2	14	14 generations of the Church Age
Day 8	1	1	7	Final 7 years before Christ returns

The Feast of Tabernacles which is seen in the chart will have its fulfillment in the future in the second coming of Christ. The bull is a burden bearing animal that was used for labor and represents strength. In this feast the bull represents the labor of the servants of Christ. The closer we get to the second coming of Christ, the amount of time laboring for the Lord decreases and can be seen in the decrease of the number of bulls sacrificed with each progressing day of the feast. As the feast progressed, the number of bulls sacrificed decreased, just as the church age progresses, there will be less days to labor for Christ. The ram represents consecration and obedience to the Father's will. When Abraham was about to sacrifice his only son Isaac on the altar, God provided a substitute with a ram. Jesus was fully consecrated to the Father's will when He became our substitute for the penalty of sin. The number of rams offered remains the same for the first seven days of the feast because Christ's consecration to the Father never changes. The last day of the Feast of Tabernacles was a sacred assembly and the one ram is the Son of God who was our substitute for sin. The lamb in the third column of the chart represents the sacrifice. Jesus Christ was our sacrificial lamb, and the Passover was celebrated on the fourteenth day when the lamb was slaughtered. The number fourteen is also the number of generations that separate Abraham to David, from David to the Babylonian captivity, and from the Babylonian captivity to Christ. "So all the generations from Abraham to David are fourteen generations, from David until the captivity in Babylon are fourteen generations, and from the captivity in Babylon until the Christ are fourteen generations" (Matthew 1:17). The number of lambs sacrificed on the eighth and final day of the feast was seven instead of fourteen. This is the last seven years prior to Christ's return. It is the seven years of the Tribulation that the Antichrist is ruling.

Taken from Scripture, this next chart gives the approximate calendar year that the people mentioned in Scripture lived, the number of generations that spanned the time frame, the total number of years these generations spanned, and the total years for that entire age.

Year	People	Generations	Years	Age	Scripture
4000 B.C.	Adam-Noah	10	1000		
3000 B.C.				2000 years Age of the Forefathers	Genesis Chapter 5 Chapter 11
3000 B.C. 2000 B.C.	Noah-Abraham	10	1000		
2000 B.C. 1000 B.C.	Abraham-David	14	1000		Matthew 1:17
1000 B.C. 605 B.C.	David-Captivity	14	395	2000 years Age of God's Chosen People	Daniel 1:1
605 B.C. 1 A.D.	Babylon-Christ	14	605		
A.D. 32-33	Church	14			Acts 2
	Church	14			Numbers 29
				2000 years Age of the Church	
	Church	14			
	Church	14			
	Tribulation	7		7 years before Christ's return	Daniel 12

Chronologically, the first two sets of ten generations from Adam to Abraham and the first three sets of fourteen generations from Abraham to Christ have been fulfilled. The next four sets of fourteen generations would be the church age and the last seven years would be the Tribulation before Christ returns. The Feast of Tabernacles cannot find its historical fulfillment until Jesus Christ returns. The church continues to labor as servants of Christ for the ingathering of souls. When the four sets of fourteen generations have been completed for the church age, then we will enter into the final seven years and Christ will return and set up His millennial reign. From Scripture it can be calculated that there are two thousand years between the birth of Adam and the birth of Abraham. Between Abraham and Jesus Christ there is also a two-thousand-year span. The only time period that Scripture is silent upon is the number of years of the church age, but the Feast of Tabernacles indicates there are four sets of fourteen generations that make up the church age. It is reasonable to suggest that the church age could also be a two-thousand-year span. There were two sets of ten generations that made up the two thousand years between Adam and Abraham because the lifespan of people was much longer. The three sets of fourteen generations that made up the two thousand years from Abraham to Jesus accounts for the fact that people began to live shorter lives after Abraham. Therefore, the four sets of fourteen generations of the church age could easily cover two thousand years because the lifespan of man has continued to decrease. The church age began at Pentecost which was fifty days after Christ's resurrection. Scholars place Jesus' crucifixion and resurrection between A.D. 32 and A.D. 33 calculating the date from the gospel of Luke. "Now in the fifteenth year of the reign of Tiberius Caesar, Pontius Pilate being governor of Judea, Herod being tetrarch of Galilee, his brother Philip tetrarch of Iturea and the region of Trachonitis, and Lysanias tetrarch of Abilene, while Annas and Caiaphas were high priests, the word of God came to John the son of Zacharias in the wilderness. And he went into all the region around the Jordan, preaching a baptism of repentance for the remission of sins" (Luke 3:1–3). John the Baptist began his ministry in the fifteenth year of the reign of Tiberius Caesar. It is a historical fact that Tiberius Caesar began his reign on August 19, A.D. 14. The fifteenth year of his reign would have been anywhere between August 19, A.D. 29 and August 19, A.D. 30. Jesus began His ministry after John the Baptist, and from the gospel of John it can be determined that Jesus' ministry lasted approximately three years. Therefore, Jesus death, resurrection, and ascension would have been either A.D. 32 or A.D. 33, depending on how soon after John the Baptist's ministry that Jesus began His ministry. The church age would have begun in A.D. 32 or A.D. 33 at Pentecost. If in fact the church age is two thousand years, as Scripture seems to indicate through the Feasts of Tabernacles, then the second coming of Christ is not that far away. Although the Father is the only One who knows the exact day and time, Scriptures certainly tell us to be aware of the signs of the times. We need to keep our eyes on Israel, for when certain events are fulfilled, Christ is coming quickly.

REVELATION 20:1–3

> "Then I saw an angel coming down from heaven, having the key to the bottomless pit and a great chain in his hand. He laid hold of the dragon, that serpent of old, who is the Devil and Satan, and bound him for a thousand years; and he cast him into the bottomless pit, and shut him up, and set a seal on him, so that he should deceive the nations no more till the thousand years were finished. But after these things he must be released for a little while."

The Lord did a marvelous work in showing me great and mighty things regarding theses verses. It says in Scripture that God will give His children dreams and visions, and that is how the Lord chose to unfold these Scriptures to me.

> And it shall come to pass afterward
> That I will pour out My Spirit on all flesh;
> Your sons and your daughters shall prophesy,
> Your old men shall dream dreams,
> Your young men shall see visions.
> And also on My menservants and on My maidservants
> I will pour out My Spirit in those days.
> (Joel 2:28–29)

This is the Lord's message and vision that He gave to me. *"The angel that John saw coming down with the great chain and key to the bottomless pit is Michael. Go to Jude 9.* "Yet Michael the archangel, in contending with the devil, when he disputed about the body of Moses, dared not bring against him a reviling accusation, but said, "The Lord rebuke you!" (Jude 9). *"Michael is the only angel that directly confronts Satan. In the Jude Scripture, Michael had to bide his time and not directly rebuke Satan. But Michael knew there would come a day when I would permit him to place Satan in chains and cast him into the bottomless pit. As with all your enemies, you must allow Me to take vengeance on them; for vengeance is Mine and I will repay. Close your eyes and I will show you a vision of Michael rebuking the devil, that serpent of the sea. Child, I want you to include the conversation between Michael and Satan because it will expose Satan's tactics and reveal that I am the answer."* This is what I saw and heard in the vision that the Lord gave me. I saw Michael's white robe and around his waist was a gold belt and attached to his belt was a key. In his hand was a chain with large thick links, approximately six inches for each link. I saw Michael coming down from heaven and I saw a veiled view of Satan that revealed his ugliness. Satan was black with what looked like large semi-transparent black wings on his back. There were visible black veins running through the wings, almost like a bat's wing, but much larger. He was hunched over and his face was so vile and ugly. He had black scraggily hair, long like a woman's but ratty and sporadic on his head. His teeth were sharp and jagged and protruded out of his mouth in jagged rows like shark's teeth. His skin was dark greenish black with a slimy appearance. He had sharp clawlike hands. I saw Michael approaching him with the large chain and Satan began to make biting movements with his teeth to try and frighten Michael. Satan's black eyes were full of venom as he spat out these words: "Ah, Michael, I see you have come. Do you think you can take me this time, my friend? How many times have we fought and you have never had the victory?" Then Michael responded to Satan, "I am not your friend! Our battles have been fierce in the past, but this time the Lord has pronounced your complete defeat. Did you think that you could rebel against the Almighty and All-powerful God and win? You thought you could strategize and manipulate people to war against the Lord of lords and King of kings, but your plan has failed!" After this conversation between Satan and Michael, I saw Michael grab Satan and wrap him in the large chain. Satan was cursing the name of God as Michael took off in flight with Satan on a chain. His destination was the bottomless pit.

Satan spewed out the same accusations to the believer that he spat out to Michael: "How many times have you battled with that sin and never had the victory?" Jesus Christ pronounced that you have victory over all sin because He died on the cross to break the power of sin. Watchman Nee in his book, *Spiritual Man*, says this:

> Romans 6 lays the foundation for the Christian deliverance from sin. Such deliverance God provides for every believer; all may enter in. Moreover, let us be unmistakably clear that this liberation from the power of sin may be experienced the very hour a sinner accepts the Lord Jesus as Savior and is born anew. He need not be a long-time believer and undergo numerous defeats before he can receive this gospel. Delay in accepting the gospel according to Romans 6 is due either to the incomplete gospel he has heard or to his unwillingness in wholly accepting and fully yielding to it. The Lord Jesus in going to the cross took with Him not only our sins but also our beings. Paul enunciates this fact by proclaiming "that our old man has been crucified with Him." Many saints upon hearing the truth of co-death, immediately assume that they ought to die, and so they try their best to crucify themselves. This is a grievous misjudgment. The Bible never instructs us to crucify ourselves. Scripture assures us that our old man was dealt with at the time Christ went to the cross. It is because we are in Him and are united with Him that we can say that when Christ went to the cross we went there with Him, that when Christ was crucified, we too were crucified in Him. What a wonderful reality that we are in Christ! The Spirit of God must reveal how we are in Christ and how we are united with Him in one. He must also show us distinctly how our old man was crucified with Christ for the simple reason that we are in Christ. This cannot be simply a mental comprehension; it must be a disclosure of the Holy Spirit. When a truth is unfolded by God, it most naturally becomes a power in man, who then finds himself able to believe. Faith comes

> through revelation. Therefore, pray until God gives us the revelation that "our old man has been crucified with Him." Sin can no longer tempt the believer for he is a new man; the old has died. But if we persist in holding onto something which God wants us to relinquish, sin shall have dominion over us. If we fail to yield our members as godly instruments of righteousness to speak and do what He desires and go where He directs, should we be surprised we are not delivered from sin? Whenever we fail to relinquish or offer resistance to God sin shall return to its dominion. Any defeat that results in sin is due either to lack of faith that we have been delivered from the power of sin or a failure to obey God.

Regarding sin, there needs to be a continual confession so that there is a continual cleansing to maintain that close intimate relationship with the Lord. The closer you get to the Lord Jesus in your relationship to Him, the more clearly you see yourself as a wretch. You become conscious that there is absolutely nothing good inside yourself; accept what Jesus Christ brings to you. You realize just how imperfect you are compared to His perfection. This awareness is not so you beat yourself up and bring self-condemnation, but to see more clearly the gift of forgiveness that Jesus brings to our daily lives and how He clothes us with His perfection. There is great freedom in being covered in His perfection and receiving His forgiveness. It allows you to move on when you blatantly sin because of disobedience, unintentionally mess up, or let your flesh control your spirit. Instead of beating yourself up over your sin, you acknowledge that the beaten body of Christ removes your sin when you ask for His forgiveness. I am in no way promoting cheap grace whereby a person has a nonchalant attitude toward sin because of Jesus' everlasting forgiveness. When you truly have a grasp of the great price that Jesus paid for your sins, it eliminates cheap grace. When you have an intimate walk with the Lord, you permit your life to be fine-tuned by the Holy Spirit. Your spirit has been trained by the Holy Spirit to recognize even the smallest things that offend God. You realize that God looks to the heart, to motives, and to thoughts, not to the outside. This is where the filthiness of sin causes you to cry out: "I have sinned against you alone, God. Please forgive me."

When you confess your sins to Jesus, the weight of guilt is lifted, the burden is removed, and the power of sin is broken. The longer you wait to confess your sin to the Lord, the heavier the burden becomes until it crushes you. King David understood the crushing weight of his sin before it was exposed. For over a year his adultery with Bathsheba and his murder of Uriah was hidden. The entry of sin into David's life and the progression of his sin are forever written in the annals of the Holy Bible. David's path of sin began in Second Samuel 10, when he experienced severe rejection by Hanun of Ammon. Hanun's father had just died and David sent delegates to console him because David had a special relationship with Hanun's father. In response to David's kindness, Hanun took David's servants and shaved half of their heads and cut their garments in the middle and sent them away. As a result of Hanun's action, war broke out between Israel and Ammon. It was this war which David stayed home from out of self-pity because his generous act of compassion towards Hanun was rejected. This rejection turned into self-pity and opened the door for a spirit to come in—the spirit of lust. Once this spirit came in through the back door because of rejection, it waited for an opportune moment to tempt. It was not by chance that David arose in the middle of the night to walk out on his roof when he should have been away fighting the war. The bait was set because Bathsheba was bathing and David viewed her. David's eyes saw the naked body of another man's wife and he began to dwell on what he saw. Then he acted on his lustful thoughts by summoning Bathsheba to the palace, knowing that it was his plan to seduce her. David sent her back home thinking that no one would ever know about his liaison because her husband and all the men were fighting the war. Then things got complicated.

Bathsheba sent word to David that she was pregnant and they both knew that something had to be done to cover up their adultery. David summoned Uriah home from the war and told him to go to his wife, presuming that any husband that had been separated from his wife for months would desire to reunite with her. This would solve the pregnancy issue and no one would really know who the real father was—except David, Bathsheba, and God! The next complication to this web of deceit and adultery came when Uriah refused to go to his wife out of loyalty to the other men in battle. He could not engage in such pleasure when his fellow countrymen were risking their lives in battle. David sent Uriah back to the battlefield and had to rethink his strategy to cover his sin of adultery which was punishable by death. David instructed his commander Joab to put Uriah on the front line of a heated battle and then withdraw the troops so that Uriah would be killed. It seemed like the perfect plan because no one would suspect that Uriah's death was actually murder, especially not Bathsheba. After Uriah's death, David took Bathsheba to be his wife and she gave birth to their son. Temporarily his sin was hidden, but not from God! Along came Nathan the prophet who exposed the whole sordid mess and pronounced God's judgment for David's sin. David paid a high price for his sin when the Lord struck their child with a sickness and he died. David would also pay another dear price for his sin. "Thus says the LORD: 'Behold, I will raise up adversity against you from your own house; and I will take your wives before your eyes and give them to your neighbor, and he shall lie with your wives in the sight of this sun. For you did it secretly, but I will do this thing before all Israel, before the sun'" (2 Samuel 12:11–12). This was fulfilled when David's son Absalom committed treason by forcefully taking David's throne. On top of the roof of the palace, in full view of all Israel, Absalom fornicated with David's concubines. The roof of the palace is where David's sin began and the roof of the palace is where his sin had its final punishment. When Absalom was killed for his treason, David wept and bemoaned his death because he knew that it was his sin with Bathsheba that robbed him of yet another son. The sequence of David's transgression shows just how deadly hidden sin really is and also identifies the entry of the spirit of lust. This sequence can also be traced to infidelities that occur with men and women as a result of rejection.

1. Rejection – cruel treatment, betrayal, abandonment, divorce, broken engagement, infidelity.
2. Self-Pity – emotion that develops because of rejection that permits spirits to enter. It especially opens the door to lust when the rejection is from an intimate partner.
3. Enticement – the man's eyes view a beautiful woman, or he permits unholy sights into the eye gate such as pornography. Enticement for the woman is when her eyes notice the look of desire from a man and the attention paid her.
4. Dwelling - lustful thoughts and fantasies about the woman or man.
5. Acting – meeting with the woman or man, committing adultery.
6. Covering – hiding the adultery with lies and deceit.
7. Committing - sins to maintain the deception.
8. Crushing – the weight of the sin taking its toll through guilt.
9. Confessing - repenting of the sin.
10. Paying - severe penalty for the sin.

At any time during this progression of sin, David could have chosen to confess his sin to God and the penalty would not have been as severe. There would have been a different outcome if David would have confessed his sin when he first viewed the naked woman. The sooner you confess any sin to Jesus, the progression and power of that sin is broken. Do not wait until you have to pay such a high price for your sin. You have a choice regarding sin; either confess it and repent, or let it progress until the Lord uncovers it. Make no mistake, He will uncover it and there will be a price you have to pay. Cry out to God as David did in this Psalm after his sin was uncovered, but do not wait as long as David did.

> Have mercy upon me, O God,
> According to Your lovingkindness;
> According to the multitude of Your tender mercies,
> Blot out my transgressions.
> Wash me thoroughly from my iniquity,
> And cleanse me from my sin.
> For I acknowledge my transgressions,
> And my sin is always before me.
> Against You, You only, have I sinned,
> And done this evil in Your sight— that You may be found just when You speak,
> And blameless when You judge.
> Behold, I was brought forth in iniquity,
> And in sin my mother conceived me.
> Behold, You desire truth in the inward parts,
> And in the hidden part You will make me to know wisdom.
> Purge me with hyssop, and I shall be clean;
> Wash me, and I shall be whiter than snow.
> Make me hear joy and gladness,
> That the bones You have broken may rejoice.
> Hide Your face from my sins,
> And blot out all my iniquities.
> (Psalm 51:1–9)

REVELATION 20:4–6

> And I saw thrones, and they sat on them, and judgment was committed to them. Then I saw the souls of those who had been beheaded for their witness to Jesus and for the word of God, who had not worshiped the beast or his image, and had not received

> his mark on their foreheads or on their hands. And they lived and reigned with Christ for a thousand years. But the rest of the dead did not live again until the thousand years were finished. This is the first resurrection. Blessed and holy is he who has part in the first resurrection. Over such the second death has no power, but they shall be priests of God and of Christ, and shall reign with Him a thousand years.

During the time that Satan is bound in the bottomless pit, Jesus Christ rules and reigns from the Holy City of Jerusalem on earth. Those that were martyred for their witness of Jesus Christ and for the word of God will also come back and reign with Jesus during this millennial reign. All those who have been called, chosen, and found faithful will have a part in the first resurrection and will come back and reign with Jesus. The Holy Spirit gave me a small glimpse of Jesus' millennial reign in this vision. First I saw a Star of David, the six-pointed star that is the national symbol of Israel. Then I saw a lone man walking down a dirt road. He stopped and looked over his shoulder, but no one was following him. By the Spirit of God I knew this man was Jesus. Then the vision changed and I saw silver bells attached to the hoofs of many horses. The bells were engraved with these words: "Holiness to the Lord." The horses were marching in unison and the bells were tinkling as they marched. I did not hear the sound of the hoofs hitting the ground, I only heard the sound of the bells and they were making a melody, a beautiful sound. The horses were so beautiful that I saw in this vision. Some of the horses were dappled, some with pure shiny black coats, some were brown with white necks, some were black with white markings, some had a smattering of brown with white and looked like an artist took a brush and randomly brushed the color in streaks, and some were all white with solid black manes. These horses were very beautiful and splendid. This whole army of horses and riders were being led by one very magnificent pure white majestic horse. This white horse was larger than all the other horses and upon this horse sat one who was regal and whose royal garments flowed over the flanks of the horse. His posture was such that he sat with his back straight, his head held up high, and his gaze forward. He exuded all the regal qualities of a king. Then I saw people lining up on both sides of the street and they were throwing rose petals onto the street before the man on the majestic white horse. When he passed them, the people fell down to their knees and on their faces and cried out in their native tongues: "Immanuel, God is with us!" The Spirit of God revealed to me that He gave me the sequence of this vision to relay this message. *"Jesus came as a man the first time and endured the long dusty road of solitude, servitude, and suffering; but Jesus will come as King the second time and enjoy the rose strewn road of adoration, accolades, and accomplishments. This Jesus that walked down the dusty streets of Jerusalem is Yeshua, the promised Messiah of the Jews. He will return and be their King. During the millennial reign of Jesus Christ, people from all nations will come to Jerusalem and honor Him as King."* When Jesus entered Jerusalem on a colt the week of His crucifixion, the people placed palm branches before Him. During the millennial reign, Jesus will enter Jerusalem on a white stallion and people will place rose petals before Him. The Lord revealed to me the significance of both of His entrances into Jerusalem. *"The palm branches laid before Me signified that I was their coming King. When I rode into Jerusalem on that colt, I was not their King even though they cried out: "Hosanna in the highest and blessed is He who comes in the name of the Lord." Less than one week had passed when they cried out: "Crucify Him! Crucify Him!" The rose petals that will be laid before Me will signify their adoration of a royal king. When I ride into Jerusalem on that white horse, they will look upon the One they have pierced and lay rose petals before Me to acknowledge that I am their King. On that day they will cry out: "Emanuel! Emanuel!"*

REVELATION 20:7–10

Now when the thousand years have expired, Satan will be released from his prison and will go out to deceive the nations which are in the four corners of the earth, Gog and Magog, to gather them

> together to battle, whose number is as the sand of the sea. They went up on the breadth of the earth and surrounded the camp of the saints and the beloved city. And fire came down from God out of heaven and devoured them. The devil, who deceived them, was cast into the lake of fire and brimstone where the beast and the false prophet are. And they will be tormented day and night forever and ever.

During the Lord's one-thousand-year reign on earth from the Holy City of Jerusalem, there will be people who rebel against Christ. Even though Jesus is dwelling on earth, there will be unbelief and sin because God never takes away man's free will. Satan will be released from the bottomless pit to once again deceive the nations. The Battle of Gog and Magog will be very similar to the Battle of Armageddon, for the armies will gather in the Jezreel Valley once again. Ezekiel gives a detailed description of the Battle of Gog and Magog.

> Therefore, son of man, prophesy and say to Gog, "Thus says the Lord GOD: "On that day when My people Israel dwell safely, will you not know it? Then you will come from your place out of the far north, you and many peoples with you, all of them riding on horses, a great company and a mighty army. You will come up against My people Israel like a cloud, to cover the land. It will be in the latter days that I will bring you against My land, so that the nations may know Me, when I am hallowed in you, O Gog, before their eyes." Thus says the Lord GOD: "Are you he of whom I have spoken in former days by My servants the prophets of Israel, who prophesied for years in those days that I would bring you against them?
>
> "And it will come to pass at the same time, when Gog comes against the land of Israel," says the Lord GOD, "that My fury will show in My face. For in My jealousy and in the fire of My wrath

I have spoken: 'Surely in that day there shall be a great earthquake in the land of Israel, so that the fish of the sea, the birds of the heavens, the beasts of the field, all creeping things that creep on the earth, and all men who are on the face of the earth shall shake at My presence. The mountains shall be thrown down, the steep places shall fall, and every wall shall fall to the ground.' I will call for a sword against Gog throughout all My mountains," says the Lord GOD. "Every man's sword will be against his brother. And I will bring him to judgment with pestilence and bloodshed; I will rain down on him, on his troops, and on the many peoples who are with him, flooding rain, great hailstones, fire, and brimstone. Thus I will magnify Myself and sanctify Myself, and I will be known in the eyes of many nations. Then they shall know that I am the LORD." (Ezekiel 38:14–23)

In prayer, I humbly asked the Lord why Satan was released after one thousand years to deceive the nations once again. This was the Lord's response to me. *"Child, I will release Satan to use him as My hand of judgment against the rebellious people of the earth. During My reign, people will still rebel against Me without the influence of Satan's manipulation and influence. By their rebellion against Me, they have declared that Satan is their father. I choose to release Satan so he can gather his children for their punishment at the Battle of Gog and Magog. Satan will be defeated and his army destroyed by fire that comes down from My Father in Heaven. Satan will meet his final demise when he is cast into the lake of fire and brimstone where the Antichrist and the False Prophet have been tortured for the previous one thousand years."*

REVELATION 20:11–15

Then I saw a great white throne and Him who sat on it, from whose face the earth and the heaven fled away. And there was found no place for them. And I saw the dead, small and great, standing before God, and books were opened. And another book

> was opened, which is the Book of Life. And the dead were judged according to their works, by the things which were written in the books. The sea gave up the dead who were in it, and Death and Hades delivered up the dead who were in them. And they were judged, each one according to his works. Then Death and Hades were cast into the lake of fire. This is the second death. And anyone not found written in the Book of Life was cast into the lake of fire.

The Lord's explanation of His Great White Throne judgment causes me to tremble for those who have rejected Christ. These are His words spoken to me through His Spirit regarding His final judgment. *"I have judged cities, nations, and the earth, and now it is time for individuals to be judged. This is the second resurrection and all are resurrected to stand before Me. There will books that are opened and also the Book of Life is opened. All those whose names are written in the Book of Life will be rewarded for their works that have been refined with My fire and still remain. I will award crowns and various robes and gowns to My children. Another set of books will be opened for the condemned. I have recorded all their evil works as well as their good works and they will be eternally punished for their rejection of Me, along with their evil works. Every living soul will stand before My judgment seat and all will bow down and confess that I am the Lord of lords and the King of kings. Those who have rejected Me as Lord and Savior will experience the second death and they will be cast into the lake of fire and receive punishment for all eternity. Those whose names are written in the Book of Life will live forever with Me."*

Chapter Ten

New! New! New!

Revelation 21:1–8

Now I saw a new heaven and a new earth, for the first heaven and the first earth had passed away. Also there was no more sea. Then I, John, saw the holy city, New Jerusalem, coming down out of heaven from God, prepared as a bride adorned for her husband. And I heard a loud voice from heaven saying, "Behold, the tabernacle of God is with men, and He will dwell with them, and they shall be His people. God Himself will be with them and be their God. And God will wipe away every tear from their eyes; there shall be no more death, nor sorrow, nor crying. There shall be no more pain, for the former things have passed away." Then He who sat on the throne said, "Behold, I make all things new." And He said to me, "Write, for these words are true and faithful." And He said to me, "It is done! I am the Alpha and the Omega, the Beginning and the End. I will give of the fountain of the water of life freely to him who thirsts. He who overcomes shall inherit all things, and I will be his God and he shall be My son. But the cowardly, unbelieving, abominable, murderers, sexually immoral, sorcerers, idolaters, and all liars shall have their part in the lake which burns with fire and brimstone, which is the second death.

After the Great White Throne judgment, the heavens and the earth that we know will be destroyed by fire from God and the new heaven and earth will come down from heaven. The Apostle Peter describes this cataclysmic event that will occur after the one-thousand-year reign of Jesus Christ.

> But the day of the Lord will come as a thief in the night, in which the heavens will pass away with a great noise, and the elements will melt with fervent heat; both the earth and the works that are in it will be burned up. Therefore, since all these things will be dissolved, what manner of persons ought you to be in holy conduct and godliness, looking for and hastening the coming of the day of God, because of which the heavens will be dissolved, being on fire, and the elements will melt with fervent heat? Nevertheless we, according to His promise, look for new heavens and a new earth in which righteousness dwells. (2 Peter 3:10–13)

Jesus will make all things new and there will no longer be a need for the sun, moon, or stars because the glory of God the Father and Jesus will illuminate the New Jerusalem. The new earth will no longer have a sea. It is very possible that the sea is removed from the new earth because it was the habitation of Leviathan, that sea serpent called the Devil. These are the Lord's words to me regarding this Scripture. *"Man only thought that he had mastered the knowledge of the earth, the sun, the moon, the stars, and the galaxies. In one breath I remove them and behold, I make all things new. Knowledge is fleeting, but knowledge of the Holy One of God is everlasting. Pursue Me, for I am the God that reveals."*

God tabernacles with all those whose names are written in the Lamb's Book of Life and will live with them forever in the New Jerusalem. Never again will there be a tear shed, and pain and sorrow will not exist because physical death has been eradicated. This euphoric state of existence whereby God dwells with His people will be the restoration of the time in the Garden of Eden. All that was lost by the sin of the first Adam will be restored by the second Adam, Jesus Christ. Everything began with Jesus and will end with Jesus, for he is the Alpha and the Omega, the Beginning and the End. Jesus is the Eternal One. To all who believe that Jesus Christ is the Son of God who died on the cross for all their sin, who rose from the dead on the third day, who confess their sins and ask Jesus to be the Lord and Savior of their lives; they will live forever with Him in the New Jerusalem. Those unbelievers who were resurrected during the second resurrection will stand before Christ and receive their punishment, which is being cast into the lake of fire and brimstone. Isaiah describes this horrible second death of those who refused Jesus. "And they shall go forth and look upon the corpses of the men who have transgressed against Me. For their worm does not die, and their fire is not quenched. They shall be an abhorrence to all flesh" (Isaiah 66:24).

REVELATION 21:9–21

> Then one of the seven angels who had the seven bowls filled with the seven last plagues came to me and talked with me, saying, "Come, I will show you the bride, the Lamb's wife." And he carried me away in the Spirit to a great and high mountain, and showed me the great city, the holy Jerusalem, descending out of heaven from God, having the glory of God. Her light was like a most precious stone, like a jasper stone, clear as crystal. Also she had a great and high wall with twelve gates, and twelve angels at the gates, and names written on them, which are the names of the twelve tribes of the children of Israel: three gates on the east, three gates on the north, three gates on the south, and three gates on the west. Now the wall of the city had twelve foundations, and on them were the names of the twelve apostles of the Lamb. And he who talked with me had a gold reed to measure the city, its gates, and its wall. The city is laid out as a square; its length is as great as its breadth. And he measured the city with the reed: twelve thousand furlongs. Its length, breadth, and height are equal. Then

> he measured its wall: one hundred and forty-four cubits, according to the measure of a man, that is, of an angel. The construction of its wall was of jasper; and the city was pure gold, like clear glass. The foundations of the wall of the city were adorned with all kinds of precious stones: the first foundation was jasper, the second sapphire, the third chalcedony, the fourth emerald, the fifth sardonyx, the sixth sardius, the seventh chrysolite, the eighth beryl, the ninth topaz, the tenth chrysoprase, the eleventh jacinth, and the twelfth amethyst. The twelve gates were twelve pearls: each individual gate was of one pearl. And the street of the city was pure gold, like transparent glass.

John was given a vision of the Holy City of the New Jerusalem that descended down from heaven and this will be God's habitation with His people for all eternity. The New Jerusalem is described by John in detail. The city is a cube that is 12,000 furlongs in length, width, and height. The original Hebrew word for this measurement is *stadion.* In the ancient Olympiad, the *stadion* was a foot race that was run by men in a facility that was also called a *stadion.* The *stadion* was approximately a 200-yard foot race; therefore 12,000 *stadion* would be close to 1363 miles. The New Jerusalem's measurements will be approximately 1363 miles in length, width, and height. The city will be surrounded by a wall made of jasper that is 144 cubits. One cubit is a measurement from a man's elbow to his fingertips which is approximately eighteen inches, so this wall will be approximately 216 feet high. On each of the four great walls surrounding the city will be three gates, totaling twelve gates. Each of these gates will be made from a single pearl and have the twelve tribes of Israel inscribed on them. Ezekiel was also given a prophecy regarding the measurements of each of those gates in the New Jerusalem.

> These are the exits of the city. On the north side, measuring four thousand five hundred cubits (the gates of the city shall be named

> after the tribes of Israel), the three gates northward: one gate for Reuben, one gate for Judah, and one gate for Levi; on the east side, four thousand five hundred cubits, three gates: one gate for Joseph, one gate for Benjamin, and one gate for Dan; on the south side, measuring four thousand five hundred cubits, three gates: one gate for Simeon, one gate for Issachar, and one gate for Zebulun; on the west side, four thousand five hundred cubits with their three gates: one gate for Gad, one gate for Asher, and one gate for Naphtali. All the way around shall be eighteen thousand cubits; and the name of the city from that day shall be: THE LORD IS THERE. (Ezekiel 48:30–35)

According to Ezekiel, each gate will measure 1500 cubits, so each of these gates will be 2250 feet wide, which is a little over four-tenths of a mile. Ezekiel also says that the names of the original tribes of Israel will be inscribed on these gates in the New Jerusalem, and the tribe of Dan is not omitted. God's mercy and grace are once again evident because He does not hold the sins of the Antichrist against the entire tribe of Dan in the end. The walls with the gates that surround the New Jerusalem also have twelve foundations made up of various gemstones. Written on each of the twelve foundations are the names of the twelve apostles. The very same gemstones that God instructed Moses to place on the breastplate of the High Priest's garment that represented the twelve tribes of Israel, are the exact gemstones that are mentioned for the foundation of the wall of the New Jerusalem. These gemstones will make up the foundation of the wall and will be such a beautiful splash of brilliant color. Jasper is red, yellow, or brown opaque quartz, the sapphire is a transparent rich blue gem, the chalcedony is a translucent pale blue quartz, the emerald is a bright green beryl, the sardonyx is a pale green beryl, the sardius is a ruby or garnet, the chrysolite is a gold stone or a diamond, the beryl is a green, yellow, pink, or white silicate, the topaz is a brilliant yellow transparent silicate, the chrysoprase is a striped quartz, the jacinth is a gem of deep blue color, and the amethyst is a quartz of clear purple or bluish purple. This array of color and beauty will truly be a magnificent sight as the glory of God shines through these walls made of precious gemstones that produce a rainbow of color. It is no wonder that the throne of God is described as having a rainbow around it. "Immediately I was in the Spirit; and behold, a throne set in heaven, and One sat on the throne. And He who sat there was like a jasper and a sardius stone in appearance; and there was a rainbow around the throne, in appearance like an emerald" (Revelation 4:2–3).

REVELATION 21:22–27

> But I saw no temple in it, for the Lord God Almighty and the Lamb are its temple. The city had no need of the sun or of the moon to shine in it, for the glory of God illuminated it. The Lamb is its light. And the nations of those who are saved shall walk in its light, and the kings of the earth bring their glory and honor into it. Its gates shall not be shut at all by day (there shall be no night there). And they shall bring the glory and the honor of the nations into it. But there shall by no means enter it anything that defiles, or causes an abomination or a lie, but only those who are written in the Lamb's Book of Life.

In the New Jerusalem there will be no need for a temple, because Jesus Christ died once and for all our sins, and His sacrifice is complete and sufficient. The glory of God the Father and Jesus Christ will light up the glorious city. "The sun shall no longer be your light by day, nor for brightness shall the moon give light to you; but the LORD will be to you an everlasting light, and your God your glory" (Isaiah 60:19). This beautiful city is the consummation of God's goodness towards all those who loved and served Jesus Christ. The Lord caused me to ponder in awe when He said this. *"The New Jerusalem is like no other city ever seen on the earth, for it is from heaven. My servant John only saw in part the glory of the New Jerusalem; for no eye has seen nor ear has heard what the Lord has in store for those who love Him."*

Revelation 22:1–5

> And he showed me a pure river of water of life, clear as crystal, proceeding from the throne of God and of the Lamb. In the middle of its street, and on either side of the river, was the tree of life, which bore twelve fruits, each tree yielding its fruit every month. The leaves of the tree were for the healing of the nations. And there shall be no more curse, but the throne of God and of the Lamb shall be in it, and His servants shall serve Him. They shall see His face, and His name shall be on their foreheads. There shall be no night there: They need no lamp nor light of the sun, for the Lord God gives them light. And they shall reign forever and ever.

John saw a river flowing from the throne of the Father and the throne of Jesus in the New Jerusalem. Along the banks of the river will be the tree of life that will bear twelve fruits every month. This is the same tree of life that was in the Garden of Eden that Adam and Eve were denied access to once they sinned. The reestablishment of the tree of life in the New Jerusalem will produce eternal life for all who partake of it. Ezekiel was also given a vision of the river flowing from the throne of God and the tree of life.

> Then he brought me back to the door of the temple; and there was water, flowing from under the threshold of the temple toward the east, for the front of the temple faced east; the water was flowing from under the right side of the temple, south of the altar....
>
> When I returned, there, along the bank of the river, were very many trees on one side and the other. Then he said to me: "This water flows toward the eastern region, goes down into the valley, and enters the sea. When it reaches the sea, its waters are healed. And it shall be that every living thing that moves, wherever the rivers go, will live. There will be a very great multitude of fish, because these waters go there; for they will be healed, and everything will

> live wherever the river goes. It shall be that fishermen will stand by it from En Gedi to En Eglaim; they will be places for spreading their nets. Their fish will be of the same kinds as the fish of the Great Sea, exceedingly many. But its swamps and marshes will not be healed; they will be given over to salt. Along the bank of the river, on this side and that, will grow all kinds of trees used for food; their leaves will not wither, and their fruit will not fail. They will bear fruit every month, because their water flows from the sanctuary. Their fruit will be for food, and their leaves for medicine. (Ezekiel 47:1, 7–12)

According to Ezekiel's description, this river of life will flow east and then enter into the Dead Sea which will be healed and be able to sustain all varieties of fish. I have been in the Dead Sea and this will truly be a miraculous healing of the waters that are currently thirty percent saline. The floor of the Dead Sea is so thick with salt and minerals that you can scoop the salt crystals by the handfuls, just as you would sand on the ocean floor. This highly concentrated Salt Sea will be transformed into a body of water that will sustain life by the healing waters that flow from the throne of God. Along the banks of this river that flows into the Dead Sea will be a variety of trees whose fruit will be for food and the leaves to maintain health and wholeness.

In the New Jerusalem, people will see Jesus face to face and His name will forever be written on their foreheads. The Lord instructed the people of Israel through Moses to bind the word of the Lord on their hands and foreheads so they would constantly be reminded to love and obey God. The Lord, having a perfect view into the New Jerusalem, knew that those who chose to love Him with all of their heart, soul, and strength would have His name written on their foreheads. This Scripture was a glimpse of the events that would take place in the New Jerusalem.

> Hear, O Israel: The LORD our God, the LORD is one! You shall love the LORD your God with all your heart, with all your soul,

> and with all your strength. "And these words which I command you today shall be in your heart. You shall teach them diligently to your children, and shall talk of them when you sit in your house, when you walk by the way, when you lie down, and when you rise up. You shall bind them as a sign on your hand, and they shall be as frontlets between your eyes. You shall write them on the doorposts of your house and on your gates. (Deuteronomy 6:4–9)

The Lord said this to me: *"I watch over Israel for she is Mine. Pray that Israel will fulfill her duties to Me. Pray that Israel will love Me with all her heart, with all her soul, and with all her strength."*

REVELATION 22:6–21

> Then he said to me, "These words are faithful and true." And the Lord God of the holy prophets sent His angel to show His servants the things which must shortly take place. "Behold, I am coming quickly! Blessed is he who keeps the words of the prophecy of this book." Now I, John, saw and heard these things. And when I heard and saw, I fell down to worship before the feet of the angel who showed me these things. Then he said to me, "See that you do not do that. For I am your fellow servant, and of your brethren the prophets, and of those who keep the words of this book. Worship God." And he said to me, "Do not seal the words of the prophecy of this book, for the time is at hand. He who is unjust, let him be unjust still; he who is filthy, let him be filthy still; he who is righteous, let him be righteous still; he who is holy, let him be holy still." "And behold, I am coming quickly, and My reward is with Me, to give to every one according to his work. I am the Alpha and the Omega, the Beginning and the End, the First and the Last. Blessed are those who do His commandments, that they may have the right to the tree of life, and may

> enter through the gates into the city. But outside are dogs and sorcerers and sexually immoral and murderers and idolaters, and whoever loves and practices a lie. "I, Jesus, have sent My angel to testify to you these things in the churches. I am the Root and the Offspring of David, the Bright and Morning Star." And the Spirit and the bride say, "Come!" And let him who hears say, "Come!" And let him who thirsts come. Whoever desires, let him take the water of life freely. For I testify to everyone who hears the words of the prophecy of this book: If anyone adds to these things, God will add to him the plagues that are written in this book; and if anyone takes away from the words of the book of this prophecy, God shall take away his part from the Book of Life, from the holy city, and from the things which are written in this book. He who testifies to these things says, "Surely I am coming quickly." Amen. Even so, come, Lord Jesus! The grace of our Lord Jesus Christ be with you all. Amen.

For the second time during this spiritual experience, John was so overwhelmed that he fell down and worshipped the angel. The angel quickly told John not to worship him because God is the only One worthy of worship. People that are used mightily by God must always be careful not to receive the praises and accolades that belong to God alone. People that God chooses to be His servants must always shift the attention away from them and lead people to glorify God for His mighty works of salvation, deliverance, and healing. Although God chooses to use people to be His vessels in fulfilling His mighty works, His Word is adamant that "no flesh should glory in His presence" (1 Corinthians 1:29).

For the second time in the Book of Revelation, a blessing was issued to those who hear and obey the prophecies within the book and to those who actively live out the commandments of God. Jesus identified Himself as the Alpha and the Omega, the Beginning and the End, the Root and Offspring of David, and the Bright and Morning Star so that the reader would have no doubt that it was the Messiah speaking. The Jewish people knew that their God was eternal, that the Messiah would come through the line of David, and that He would be a Ruler of Israel. Jesus wanted to make sure that all who read the book of Revelation would have no doubt that He is the Messiah and that His return is imminent. Twice, Jesus said to John that He is coming quickly. Since the book of Revelation was written in A.D. 96 and we are currently in the year 2009, one might think that Jesus' words are not accurate. Not so! Man's concept of time and God's time are definitely not the same. "But, beloved, do not forget this one thing, that with the Lord one day is as a thousand years, and a thousand years as one day" (2 Peter 3:8). According to God's timetable, two days have not yet been completed since the writing of Revelation!

This revelation that Jesus Christ gave to John was so important to the church that a severe warning was issued regarding the contents of the book. Anyone who altered this book by adding or removing the written word would be a recipient of the horrific plagues and his name would be blotted out of the Lamb's Book of Life. The curse for altering this book in any manner would mean eternal death in hell! Could it be that during the seven years of the Tribulation, the apostate church will alter the book of Revelation to further deceive the people so they will take the mark of the Beast?

These were the Lord's final words that He gave to me regarding His great book of Revelation. *"I have given you the Book of Revelation because I AM THE GOD WHO REVEALS! Hear, O Israel, the Lord your God is One God. Hear, O Church, the Lord your God is One God. I am the God of Israel first and the God of the Gentiles second. The time is coming when the number of Gentiles to be grafted in will reach its fullness and then the Olive Tree will flourish. Hear, O Church, the time is short to complete your mission to go to the ends of the earth with My gospel. The final Great Harvest is about to commence. First, I will permit plagues, wars, pestilence, earthquakes, and famine. My Church, do not be discouraged by these, for they must occur before the final Great Harvest. When man can no longer rely on man, many will turn to Me. I have prepared work for you to do in advance. Many are called but few are chosen because they refuse to walk in the fullness of My calling. Laboring for the Master requires sacrifice, suffering, and obedience, and I will abundantly reward those who answer My call. My Church, much work needs to be done. He who has an ear let him hear what the Spirit says to the churches. BEHOLD, I AM COMING QUICKLY!"*

Reference List

King James Version Bible Public Domain.

Nee, Watchman, *The Spiritual Man, Volume One* (New York: Christian Fellowship Publishers, 1968, 1977), 131-138.

New King James Version Bible (Tennessee: Thomas Nelson Publishers, 1982).

Strong, James, *The New Strong's Exhaustive Concordance of the Bible* (Tennessee: Thomas Nelson Publishers, 1995, 1996).

http://www.nasa.gov/centers/dryden/research/X45/index.html August 2, 2008.